If I Had a
MILLION DOLLARS

Napoleon Hill (1883–1970), best known for his global bestseller *Think and Grow Rich*, was a self-help author and businessman whose work has influenced millions across the world, from Norman Vincent Peale to Donald Trump. Born poor, Hill lived a colourful life, pursuing several different business ventures and professions. He also met and advised many famous people, such as US President Woodrow Wilson. Hill eventually found widespread success as a motivational author, writing several books on how to achieve success and practically creating the self-help genre.

If I Had a
MILLION DOLLARS

Strategies to **Think** *and* **Grow Rich**

NAPOLEON HILL

RUPA

Published by
Rupa Publications India Pvt. Ltd 2024
7/16, Ansari Road, Daryaganj
New Delhi 110002

Sales centres:
Bengaluru Chennai
Hyderabad Jaipur Kathmandu
Kolkata Mumbai Prayagraj

Edition copyright © Rupa Publications India Pvt. Ltd 2024

All rights reserved.
No part of this publication may be reproduced, transmitted,
or stored in a retrieval system, in any form or by any means, electronic,
mechanical, photocopying, recording or otherwise, without the prior
permission of the publisher.

P-ISBN: 978-93-5702-880-6
E-ISBN:978-93-5702-759-5

First impression 2024

10 9 8 7 6 5 4 3 2 1

Printed in India

This book is sold subject to the condition that it shall not, by way of
trade or otherwise, be lent, resold, hired out, or otherwise circulated,
without the publisher's prior consent, in any form of binding or
cover other than that in which it is published.

CONTENTS

1. The Beginning of All Riches — 7
2. Positive Mental Attitude — 17
3. The Basic Attitude That Brings Wealth and Peace of Mind — 39
4. Going the Extra Mile — 54
5. Organized Planning — 74
6. Self Control — 89
7. Will You Master Money? Or Will It Master You? — 92
8. How to Develop Your Own Healthy Ego — 108
9. Concentration — 124
10. The Habit of Saving — 143
11. Cultivate Creative Vision — 157
12. Peace of Mind and Power of Mind — 165

1

THE BEGINNING OF ALL RICHES

The largest audience ever assembled in the history of mankind sat breathlessly awaiting the message of a mysterious man who was about to reveal to the world the secret of his riches.

In that audience were men who had tried and failed so often that they had all but lost hope!

And there were young men and young women—mere boys and girls—who were filled with hope and courage and eagerness to learn the way to riches.

There were doctors, lawyers, dentists, engineers and school teachers, waiting to hear what the speaker might have to say which would put them on the road to riches.

Clergymen of every religion on earth were there, with the hope that they might gather from the message of the speaker some inspirational ideas they could pass on to the members of their congregations.

Newspaper reporters were more numerous than bees; a great

battery of cameras trained upon the speaker's platform, and the newsreel men were present with their moving picture cameras and sound equipment.

There were taxicab drivers, mechanics, bricklayers, merchants, barbers, and newsboys, representing every trade and every calling on earth, and many of them had come from distant places.

Slowly the curtain began to rise, the Chairman walking to the speaker's dais raised his hand for silence! The noise died down and a silent hush spread over the great audience.

The introduction of the speaker was brief. The Chairman simply said, "Ladies and Gentlemen, I have the honor to introduce to you the richest man in all the world. He has come to tell you about the MASTER-KEY TO RICHES."

The speaker walked briskly to the speaker's dais.

He was dressed in a long black robe and wore a mask over his eyes.

His hair was of a grayish tint, and he appeared to be about sixty years of age.

He stood silently for a few moments, while the cameras flashed. Then, speaking slowly, in a voice soft and pleasing, like music, he began his message:

You have come here to seek the MASTER-KEY TO RICHES!

You have come because of that human urge for the better things in life, which is the common desire of all people.

You desire economic security which money alone can provide.

Some of you desire an outlet for your talents in order that you may have the joy of creating your own riches.

Some of you are seeking the easy way to riches, with the hope that you will find it without giving anything in return; that too is a common desire. But it is a desire I shall hope to modify for your benefit, as from experience I have learned that there is no such thing as something for nothing.

THE MAGIC POTION THAT LEADS TO RICHES

This MASTER-KEY is an ingenious device with which those who possess it may unlock the door to the solution of all of their problems. Its powers of magic transcend those of the famous Aladdin's Lamp.

It opens the door to sound health.

It opens the door to love and romance.

It opens the door to friendship, by revealing the traits of personality and character which make enduring friends.

It reveals the method by which every adversity, every failure, every disappointment, every mistaken error of judgment, and every past defeat may be transmuted into riches of a priceless value.

It kindles anew the dead hopes of all who possess it, and it reveals the formula by which one may "tune in" and draw upon the great reservoir of Infinite Intelligence, through that state of mind known as Faith.

It lifts humble men to positions of power, fame and fortune.

It turns back the hands of the clock of Time and renews the spirit of youth for those who have grown old too soon.

It provides the method by which one may take full and complete possession of one's own mind, thus giving one unchallengeable control over the emotions of the heart and the power of thinking.

It bridges the deficiencies of those who have inadequate education through formal schooling, and puts them substantially on the same plane of opportunity that is enjoyed by those who have a better education.

And lastly, it opens the doors, one by one, to the Twelve Great Riches of Life, which I shall presently describe for you in detail.

Listen carefully to what I have to say, for I shall not pass this way again. Listen not only with open ears, but with open minds and eager hearts, remembering that no man may hear that for which he has not the preparation for hearing.

The preparation consists of many things, among them sincerity of purpose, humility of heart, a full recognition of the truth that no man knows everything; that the combined knowledge of mankind has not been enough to save men from cutting one another to pieces through warfare, nor to restrain them from cheating and stealing the fruits of labor from their fellowmen.

I shall speak to you of facts and describe to you many principles of which many of you may never have heard, for they are known only to those who have prepared themselves to accept the MASTER-KEY—a small but ever-increasing number of people who have attained the Degree of Fellowship.

The Fellowship is made up of men and women from many walks of life, of all nationalities and creeds. Its purpose is to reveal to mankind the benefits which are available through the spirit of the Brotherhood of man.

The Fellowship was born of the necessity of rehabilitating a war-worn world into which civilization was brought to the very brink of destruction through World War II. The Fellowship is non-sectarian and noncommercial.

Its members work individually. It has no authorized leaders, but every one who qualifies for the Degree of Fellowship becomes a leader unto himself.

The only condition that is required for membership is that all who qualify for the degree shall share with others the benefits they receive through the MASTER-KEY TO RICHES—as many others as they may find who are willing to prepare themselves to receive the benefits.

The Fellowship prepares men and women to relate themselves to one another as brothers and sisters.

It recognizes the great abundance of material riches available for mankind and provides a rational plan by which every person may share in these riches in proportion to his talents, as they are expressed through useful service.

It frowns upon the idea of too much for the few and too little for the many, but it also discourages all who endeavor to get something for nothing. And it discourages the accumulation of riches by individuals whose greed inspires them to seek more than they can use for their own economic security and to provide opportunities through which others may attain such security.

The Fellowship has a stupendous task ahead of it.

Civilization must live and go forward, not backward, for that is the plan of the Creator of all things.

Men must learn to live together as brothers, so that they may walk arm in arm, do the world's work and reap their just reward without poverty, without hardship, without fear or trembling.

The members of the Fellowship have learned to do this without suffering the loss of any of the joys of living or sacrificing any of their rights as individuals. Nay, they have discovered that the Fellowship way is the only path to enduring happiness.

I have come to tell you about the Fellowship and to place in your hands the MASTER-KEY to all riches.

My identity will not be revealed, for it would be of no benefit to you. If you wish to speak of me you may call me the "Rich Man from Happy Valley."

THE DUAL SELF

Before I describe the Twelve Great Riches let me reveal to you some of the riches you already possess; riches of which most of you may not be conscious.

First, I would have you recognize that each of you is a plural personality, although you may regard yourself as a single personality. You and every other person consist of at least two distinct personalities, and many of you possess more.

There is that self which you recognize when you look into a mirror. That is your physical self. But it is only the house in which your other selves live. In that house there are two individuals at least who are eternally in conflict with each other.

One is a negative sort of person who thinks and moves and lives in an atmosphere of fear and doubt and poverty and ill health. This self expects failure, and seldom is disappointed. It thinks of the circumstances of life which you do not want but which you seem forced to accept—poverty, greed, superstition, fear, doubt, worry and physical sickness.

And one is your "other self," a positive sort of person who thinks in terms of opulence, sound health, love and friendship, personal achievement, creative vision, service to others, and who guides you unerringly to the attainment of all of these blessings. It is this self which alone is capable of recognizing and appropriating the Twelve Great Riches. It is the only self which is capable of receiving the Master-Key to Riches.

These are not imaginary personalities of which I speak. They are real, for they have been revealed through scientific investigation of irreproachable authenticity.

Then you have many other priceless assets of which you may not be aware; hidden riches you have neither recognized nor used. Among these is a modern radio broadcasting and receiving station so powerful that it may pick up and send out the vibrations of thought from or to any part of the world, including the potential capacity to reach out into the cosmos and tune in with the power of Infinite Intelligence.

Your radio station operates automatically and continuously, when you are asleep just as when you are awake.

And it is under the control at all times of one or the other of your two major personalities, the negative personality or the positive personality. When your negative personality is in control your radio station picks up only the negative thought vibrations which are being sent out by hundreds of millions of other negative personalities throughout the world. These are accepted, acted upon and translated into their physical equivalent in terms of the circumstances of life which you do not wish.

When your positive personality is in control it picks up only the positive thought vibrations being released by millions of other positive personalities throughout the world, and translates them into their physical equivalent in terms of prosperity, sound health, love, hope, faith, peace of mind and happiness; the values of life for which you and every other normal person are searching.

I have come to reveal to you the Master-Key by which you may attain these and many other riches. That mysterious key which unlocks the doors to the solution of all human problems, acquires all riches, and places every individual radio station under the control of one's "other self."

I am known as the Rich Man from Happy Valley because I have come into possession of the Master-Key to Riches. The nature of my riches I shall presently reveal to you. But first let me tell you that I was not born to riches.

I was born in poverty and illiteracy.

My formal education has been limited to the knowledge available through a country grade school.

And the entire universe, as far as I was concerned, extended no further than the boundary lines of the backwoods county into which I was born.

Then came a great awakening. Love came into my heart, and with it the influence of the greatest person I shall ever hope to know. She became my wife and guide, for she came from the outer world—that world I had not suspected to exist. She was a woman of culture and education. From her I learned some of the secrets of biology, and chemistry, and astronomy, and physics. She reached deeply into my soul and uncovered that "other self" of which I had no knowledge.

Step by step, patiently and with love, she lifted me into a higher and yet higher plane of understanding, until at long last I was prepared to receive the great Master-Key to Riches—the gift which I shall share with you in the hope that you may become as rich as I.

With that blessing came also a responsibility consisting of an obligation to reveal the secrets of the great Master-Key to as many of you as may prepare yourselves to receive it. But let me here warn you that the Master-Key may be retained only by those who accept the obligation to share it with others. No man may use it selfishly, for his personal aggrandizement alone.

I shall reveal to you the means by which you may share the blessings of the Master-Key, but the responsibility of sharing must become your own.

The founders of the Rotary Club movement must have recognized the benefits of sharing, for they adopted as their motto: "*He profits most who serves best.*"

And every close observer must have recognized that all individual successes which endure *have had their beginning through the beneficent influence of some other individual,* through some form of sharing.

My great opportunity consisted in the willingness of my wife to share with me the knowledge which she had acquired, plus the knowledge I gained from the principles which placed the Master-Key within my reach.

Your opportunity may well consist in my willingness to share this knowledge with you. But I have not come to give you material riches alone. I have come to share with you the knowledge by which you may acquire riches—*all riches*—through the expression of *your own personal initiative!*

That is the greatest of all gifts!

And it is the only kind of gift that anyone who is blessed with the advantages of a great nation like ours should expect. For here we have every potential form of riches available to mankind. We have them in great abundance.

So I assume that you too wish to become rich.

Let us become partners in the attainment of your desire, for I have found the way to all riches. Therefore I am prepared to serve as your guide.

I sought the path to riches the hard way before I learned that there is a short and dependable path I could have followed had I been guided as I hope to guide you.

Before we begin our journey to the land of riches let us take inventory so that we may know the true nature of riches. Yes, let us be prepared to recognize riches when we come within their reach.

Some believe that riches consist in money alone!

But enduring riches, in the broader sense, consist in many other values than those of material things, and may I add that without these other intangible values the possession of money will not bring the happiness which some believe it will provide.

When I speak of "riches" I have in mind the greater riches whose possessors have made life pay off on their own terms—the terms of full and complete happiness. I call these the "*Twelve Riches of Life*." And I sincerely wish to share them with all of you who are prepared to receive them, in whole or in part.

You may wonder about my willingness to share, so I shall tell you that the MASTER-KEY TO RICHES enables its possessors to add to their own store of riches everything of value which they share with others.

This is one of the strangest facts of life, but it is a fact which each of you must recognize and respect if you hope to become as rich as I.

POINTS TO REMEMBER

1. How to take full and complete possession of one's own mind.
2. The twelve great riches of life.
3. The fellowship way is the only path to enduring happiness.

2

POSITIVE MENTAL ATTITUDE

Let me tell you something that happened last Saturday. I went down to the travel agency to get my ticket changed so I could come back on Monday instead of Sunday. When I walked in, the manager of the travel agency grabbed my hand when he saw who I was, and he introduced himself and started in to selling me *Think and Grow Rich*. While he was holding my hand and talking to me, along came a friend of his who was connected with one of the airlines. When his friend heard the name Napoleon Hill, he grabbed the other hand and started to sell me *Think and Grow Rich*. He said, "You may be interested in knowing that before I went with the airline, I had a sales organization with approximately a hundred people, and I required every salesman to have all of your books. That was a must." Well, I felt pretty good. Outside, I encountered two very nice-looking young ladies standing on the sidewalk, giving out election literature. As I passed by, one of them said, "Aren't you Napoleon Hill? I was at a woman's club about two years ago when you delivered an address. This is my cousin. Both of our husbands are very successful now due to the fact they have read your books." I went on over to my car, and a policeman was making out a ticket. After all this talk, there was a payoff. You see, I put a penny in the parking meter, thinking that twelve minutes would be all I would need on the meter. But as I stopped to bathe my vanity in all this nice conversation, when I got to the meter, a policeman was halfway finished making out a ticket. He didn't know whose car it was, but I walked up to him and said, "Now, you wouldn't do that to Napoleon Hill, would you?" He said, "Who?" I said, "Napoleon Hill." He said, "No, I wouldn't do that to Napoleon Hill, but I certainly would do it to you." I showed him my credit card and my driver's license. And he said, "Well, I'll be a monkey's uncle!" He took the ticket and tore it up and said we'd just forget about that. And he said, "You may be interested in knowing that I'm on the Glendale Police Force as a result of reading your book, *Think and Grow Rich*."

> Nothing constructive and worthy of man's efforts ever has been or ever will be achieved, except that which comes from a positive mental attitude based on definiteness of purpose, activated by a burning desire, and intensified until the burning desire is elevated to the plane of applied faith.

Here are five different conditions of the mind that lead to a positive mental attitude. In other words, these five are precursors to a positive mental attitude: wishes, hopes, burning desire, applied faith, and action.

1: BEGIN WITH WISHES

Everybody has a stock of wishes. They wish for this and they wish for that and they wish for the other thing. We all have wishes. Well, nothing very much happens when you just wish for things, does it? No, nothing happens. Well, then you go a little bit further and you become curious. You put in a lot of time through idle curiosity. And do you think anything ever happens worthwhile in connection with the expression of idle curiosity? However, sometimes you can and you do consume a lot of time with idle curiosity, don't you? Sometimes, you put in a lot of time in studying what your neighbors do or not do, what your competitors do or not do, all just out of idle curiosity. That's not leading to a positive mental attitude.

2: WISHES LEAD TO HOPE

A step above wishes is hope, when your wishes take on a more concrete form. They become hopes of achievement, hopes of attainment, hopes of accomplishment, and hopes of accumulation of things that you want. However, a hope by itself is not very effective. We all have a flock of hopes, but not all of us who have hopes have success. We just hope for success. Hoping is better than wishing. Because the difference between a hope and a wish is that hope is a beginning to take on faith. That's the idea of hope. You're transmuting a wish into that very desirable state of mind known as faith.

3: HOPE FUELS BURNING DESIRE

At some point, you step up your mental attitude to where your hopes are transmuted into something else, known as a burning desire. There's a difference between a burning desire and an ordinary desire. A burning desire is an intensified desire based upon hope, and based upon definiteness of purpose. In this way, a burning desire is actually an obsessional desire, fueled by a motive. You cannot have a burning desire without a motive or motives back of it, and the more motives you can have for a definite thing, the quicker you will have turned your emotions into what is known as a burning desire. However, that's not enough. There's something else. There's another state of mind you must have before you can be sure of success.

4: APPLIED FAITH

If you have transmuted wishes, idle curiosity, hopes, and even a burning desire, you have stepped all those up into something still higher, and that is applied faith. What is the difference between applied faith and ordinary belief in things?

5: ACTION

The word *applied* might well be synonymous to *action*. You might say active faith. Applied faith and active faith are the same: faith backed by action, something that you do about it. A prayer brings positive results only when it is expressed in a positive mental attitude. The most effective prayers are those expressed by individuals who have conditioned their minds to habitually think in terms of a positive mental attitude.

BEING NEGATIVE IS EXHAUSTING!

Do you have any idea of the amount of time you devote each day in thinking of the negative side of things in comparison with the positive side? Wouldn't it be interesting if you kept a tabulation for two or three days of the exact amount of time you put into thinking about the no-can-do side of life and the can-do side, or the positive side and the negative side? Even the most successful people would be astounded to find out how many hours they spend each day in negative thinking. The very outstanding successes in the world are the ones that put in very little time, if any, thinking on the negative side. The great leaders put in all their time thinking on the positive side.

I once asked Henry Ford if there was anything in the world that he wanted or wanted to do that he couldn't do, and he said no, he didn't believe there was. I asked him if there ever had been. He said yes, back in the early days before he had learned how to use his mind. And I said, "Just what do you mean by that?" He said, "When I want a thing or want to do a thing, I start in finding out what I can do about it and start doing *that*, and I don't bother about what I can't do, because I just let that alone." There's a world of philosophy wrapped up in that statement. He put his mind into doing something about the part that he could do something about, and thinking about that, and not about the part that he couldn't do anything about.

I think if you put a problem—a difficult problem—to the majority of people, they will immediately begin to tell you all of the reasons why the problem can't be solved. And if there are some things about the problem that are favorable and some that are unfavorable, most people will see the things that are unfavorable first and often never see the favorable side. I don't believe there are any problems in which you can't do something, or in which there are no favorable sides. I can't think of a single problem that I might confront that wouldn't have a favorable side to it. If nothing else, the favorable side would be that I would say that if it's a problem I can solve, I will solve it, and if it's a problem I can't solve, I'll not worry about it. But when the majority of people are confronted with difficult propositions or problems that they can't solve, they start worrying and they go into a negative state of mind. You don't accomplish anything worthwhile when you're in that state of mind.

You're only muddying the water when you make your mind negative.

You never accomplish anything worthwhile.

To do anything worthwhile, you have to learn to keep your mind positive all the time. **A positive mental attitude attracts opportunities and a negative mental attitude repels them.** Do you think repelling opportunities has anything to do with your merit or right to have opportunities? Absolutely not. You may have the right to all of the good things in life. You may be entitled to them. But if you have a negative mental attitude, you will repel the opportunities leading to the attainment of those things. So your job is to keep your mind positive so it will attract to you the things that you want, the things that you desire, and the things that you are going after.

Have you ever stopped to think why prayer generally doesn't bring anything about—except a negative result? Have you ever stopped to wonder about that? I believe the biggest stumbling block of most people in all religions is that they don't understand why prayer sometimes brings the negative results, or why it generally brings negative results. You couldn't expect anything else, because there's a law that governs that. The law is that your mind attracts to you the counterpart of the things that the mind is feeding upon. There's no exception to that rule. It's a natural law and there are no exceptions for anybody. So if you want to attract (in prayer or otherwise) the things that you desire, you have to make your mind positive. You not only have to believe, but you have to put action back of that belief and transmute it into faith—applied faith. And you can't have applied faith in a negative state of mind; the two just don't go together.

People who recognize what a powerful influence one's daily environment has on the maintenance of a positive mental attitude often use constructive mottoes. Placing mottoes printed in large letters in all departments and changing them weekly *positivized* the entire industrial plant of the R. J. Letourneau Company, with two thousand employees. Those mottoes were written for a purpose. Every department in that great, sprawling plant of the Letourneau Company had those mottoes placed there regularly, sometimes daily in the cafeteria and weekly in the other departments. The mottoes were written in letters half a foot high so that you could read them all the way across the building. And believe me, every time they walked into their department, they saw that motto. By the way, we had a funny experience with them. I was standing in the cafeteria one day when a motto was placed up. The cafeteria was the place where all the men lined up to get their meals at noontime, and we could catch them all there at one time or another during the day. The cafeteria motto read, "Just remember that your real boss is the one who walks around under your hat." Now, I'd think that would be as plain as mud to anybody that would read it. It would mean that you're the real boss in the final analysis. But I heard a man let out an Indian yell and he said, "Boy, that's what I've always said. I've always known that my foreman was a louse."

STEPS FOR TRANSMUTATION

There is a method by which one may transmute failure into success, poverty into riches, sorrow into joy, and fear into faith.

The transmutation must start with a positive mental attitude, because success, riches, and faith do not make good bedfellows with a negative mental attitude. The transmutation procedure is simple. Here it is, and you can very well afford to come back to this many times, assimilate it, and make it your own.

1: When failure overtakes you, start thinking of it as if it had been a success. To most people this seems difficult to do but it's really not. Think of it as what would have happened if it had been a success instead of a failure. See yourself in the success side of the situation, and not in the failure side. Imagine the circumstances of the failures as being a success. Start also looking for the seed of an equivalent benefit—*which comes with every failure*—and that is where you will be able to transmute the failure into success, because every adversity, every failure, and every defeat has the seed of an equivalent benefit. If you search for that seed, you will not take a negative mental attitude toward the circumstance, you will take a positive mental attitude, because you're sure to find that seed. You may not find it the first time you look for it, but eventually you will find it, if you keep on looking for it.

2: When poverty threatens to catch up with you, or has actually caught up, start thinking of it as riches, and visualize the riches and all the things that you would wish to do with actual riches. Start looking for the seed of an equivalent benefit of poverty. I remember when I was a little boy sitting on the bank of the river down in Wise County, where I was born, just after my mother died and before my stepmother came along. I was hungry. I didn't have enough food. I was sitting there on the bank of the river wondering if I could catch some fish, maybe fry it, and have something to eat. I don't know what caused me to do this, but I shut my eyes and looked into the future. I saw myself going away, becoming famous and wealthy, and coming back to that very spot, charging up the river on a horse, a mechanical horse that was run by steam. I could see the steam pouring out his nostrils. I could hear his horseshoes clicking on the rocks. It was so vivid to me. In other words, I built myself into a state of ecstasy there in that hour of poverty, and need, and want, and hunger.

Years passed, and the time came when I drove my Rolls-Royce to that very spot, the car that I paid $22,500 for. I drove my Rolls-Royce to that very spot, and I went back and imagined again that childhood scene where I had been there in poverty, in want, and in hunger. And I said, "Well, I don't know whether my imagination back in the early days had anything to do with it or not. Maybe it did." Maybe I kept alive that hope and eventually translated that hope into faith and eventually that faith brought me not only a steam horse, but something much more valuable and much more costly than a steam horse.

Look forward and imagine the things that you want to do. Transmute unfavorable circumstances and adversities into something that's pleasant. By that, I mean switching your mind away from thinking about the unpleasant things over to something that's pleasant.

3: When fear overtakes you, remember that fear is only faith in reverse gear, and start thinking in terms of faith by seeing yourself translating faith into whatever circumstance or things you desire. I don't suppose anybody ever escapes experiencing the seven basic fears at one time or another, and most people experience them all the way through life. But if you allow fear to take possession and grip you, it will not only become a habit, it will also attract to you all of the things that you don't want. You have to learn to deal with fear by mentally transmuting it or translating it or transforming it into the opposite of fear—in other words, faith.

If you fear poverty, commence thinking of yourself in terms of opulence and of money. Think of ways and means that you're going to earn that money, acquire it, and what you'll do with it after you get it. There's no end to the daydreaming you can do; it's far better to daydream about the money you're going to have than it is to fear the poverty that you know you already have. There's no virtue and no benefit in bemoaning the fact that you are poverty-stricken or that you need money and you don't know how to get it.

There isn't anything in this world that I need that money can buy, or that anything else can buy, that I can't get if I want it. I don't think in terms of what I can't get, I think in terms of what I can get, and I've been doing that for a long time. It's wonderful to condition your mind to be positive. When the circumstances arise where you need a positive mental action, you'll be in the habit of always reacting in a positive way rather than a negative way.

You don't get a positive mental attitude just by wishing for it. You get it by weaving rope, a cord at a time, day by day, little by little. You don't just get it overnight.

HELPFUL INVISIBLE GUIDES

Create in your imagination an army of invisible guides who will take care of all your needs and all your desires—and there they are. You've heard me speak of my invisible guides, and if you weren't in this philosophy, if you didn't understand metaphysics, you'd probably say that was a very fantastic system that I've worked out. I assure you, it's not a fantastic system. I assure you that it looks after all of my needs and all of my wants. I'll admit that last week, I became a little bit careless and the guide to sound physical health let me down for a day or two. But I did something out of it. I came to his rescue. I gave him a jab in the ribs and woke him up, and believe me, I've got more energy now than I've had since we started this course. So it's a good thing that I had that little cold, because it made me express gratitude to this guide of sound physical health, not neglect him.

I fully realize that these guides are a creation of my own imagination. I'm not kidding myself or anybody else about that. But for all practical purposes, they represent real entities and real people. Each one is performing the exact duty that I assigned to him, and is doing it all the time.

GUIDE FOR PHYSICAL SOUND HEALTH

The first of these guides is the guide to physical sound health. Why do you suppose I put that as number one? What in the world could the mind do with a body that has to be supported by crutches all the time? A good, strong physical body is the temple of the mind; it has to be sound, it has to be healthy, and it has to have plenty of energy. When you turn on your enthusiasm, if there's no energy, you can't generate something out of nothing, because you've got to have a store of energy. Energy is both physical and mental in nature. I don't know of anybody who can express intense enthusiasm when their body is a series of aches and pains.

The first duty to yourself is to your physical body. See that it responds to all of your needs at all times, and does the thing that it is supposed to do. You need a little bit more help than what you can give during the day, and so when you lay your body down, nature goes to work on it, giving it a tune-up and a working over. You have to have this trained entity called the guide to sound health to do that job, to supervise it and to see that it's done properly.

GUIDE TO FINANCIAL PROSPERITY

The second most important guide is the guide to financial prosperity. Do you know of anybody that can be of great service to others without money?

How long can you get along without money? You've got to have money. You've got to have a money consciousness, and this entity that you build up through this guide gives you a money consciousness.

My guide is so controlled, however, that he doesn't make money. My God, I don't permit that! I don't permit myself to become greedy, to want an over amount of money, or to pay too much for the money that I get. I pay enough, but not too much. I know people who pay too much and who also die too young because they put too much effort into accumulating money that they didn't need and couldn't use. The only purpose it serves is that it causes their descendants to fight over it after they pass on. That's not going to happen to me. I want enough, but not too much. It's my guide's business to see that I don't want too much and that I stop when I get enough.

This money-getting business becomes a kind of a vicious circle with a lot of people. You say, "Well, I'll make my first million, then I'll quit." I remember when Bing Crosby announced to his brother (who was also his manager) that when they made their first $50,000, that would be enough and they would quit. They now make over a million dollars every year and they're still struggling in the rat race and working harder than ever. I'm not speaking in a derogatory manner. Bing's a friend of mine, and I greatly admire him. I'm referring to all people who pay too much to get things that they don't need.

This is a philosophy dealing with economic success, but success doesn't require destroying your life and dying too young because you tried to get too much of anything. Stop when you get enough. Make better use of the things you have right now, instead of trying to get a lot of more things that you're not going to make any use of at all. There's a wonderful statement in the Bible. I won't translate it verbatim, but it basically says, "Not too much, not too little of anything." Not too much, not too little—just enough of everything. Learning what is enough and not too much is one of the blessings of this philosophy. It gives you a balanced life. Learn for yourself what is enough and what's too much.

GUIDE TO PEACE OF MIND

What good is it if you owned everything in the world and collected a royalty from every living person, if you didn't have peace of mind? I've had the privilege of intimately knowing the most outstanding, the most successful, and the richest men that this country has ever produced. I've slept in their houses, ate with them, known their families, their wives, and their children. And I've seen what happened to their children after they died and passed on. I know the importance of learning to live a balanced life that lets you make your occupation (or your daily labor or whatever game that you're getting joy out of) *and* have peace of mind along the way. It's not something to be abhorred or dreaded, but a sort of game you play as ardently as a man would play a game of golf or any other game that he loves.

I have always said that one of the sins of civilization is that so few people are engaged in a labor of love, a thing that they like to do. Most people are doing things because they have to eat and sleep and have clothes to wear. Let me tell you that when a man or a woman gets in a position where he or she can do a thing for the sake of love—because they *want* to do it—they're really fortunate. This philosophy leads to that very condition, but you'll never attain that position until you learn to maintain a positive mental attitude a major portion of the time.

The men that collaborated with me in the building of this philosophy represented every outstanding success in every field of their era. Out of all of those men, there was only one that I could say even vaguely approached having peace of mind along with his other successes: John Burroughs. Without doubt, he was the one that came nearest it, and the one that came next nearest to it was Mr. Edison. I would place Mr. Carnegie as number three and I'll tell you why. In the latter part of his years, he practically lost his mind trying to find ways and means of disgorging himself of his fortune and giving it away where it would do no harm. It almost drove him crazy. His major obsession in the latter part of his days was to get this philosophy well organized while he was living and into the hands of the people. He wanted this philosophy to provide them with the know-how by which they could acquire material things, including money, without violating the rights of other people. That's what he wanted more than any other, more than anything else in the world. Unfortunately, Mr. Carnegie died in 1919, before I translated this into writing and before I wrote the first books on it. Until then, he checked (and double-checked) with me on fifteen of the seventeen principles.

There are two people that I've always regretted didn't live to see me in the day of my triumph, because they saw me in the days of my discouragement and opposition. Those two people were my stepmother and my sponsor, Andrew Carnegie. It would have been a great joy to me—and enough compensation for a lifetime of effort—if those two wonderful people could have seen the results of their handiwork in manipulating me and directing me when I needed direction. I'm not so sure that they are not looking over my shoulder now.

Sometimes I'm sure somebody is looking over my shoulder, because I say and do things that are beyond my reasonable intelligence. I have noticed, more so in recent years than ever, that the things that I do which might be called brilliant and outstanding are always done by this man who's standing here, looking over my shoulder. In any emergency that calls for making important decisions, I can almost feel that man telling me what decision to make. I can almost turn around and imagine he's standing there in person. There is an influence there; there's no two ways about it. I could never have done what has been done in connection with this philosophy if I had nothing but the collaboration of those five or six hundred men that helped me. That wouldn't have been enough. Believe me, I have had more than that. I haven't said anything about it because I don't want to make people feel that I have been favored, or that I have anything that anybody else can't have.

My honest opinion is that I don't have anything that you can't have. Whatever sources of inspiration I am drawing upon, you can have that same source. It's just as available to you as it is to me. I believe that with all of my heart.

GUIDES OF HOPE AND FAITH

I see these as twins, the guides of hope and faith. How far would you get in life if you didn't have that eternal burning flame of hope and faith working in your soul? There wouldn't be anything worth working or worth living for, would there?

You have to have a system for keeping your mind positive, as a resistance to all the things that can destroy hope and faith. People, circumstances, and all sorts of things you can't control pop up in your life. You've got to have a system as antidote to those things to offset them, something that you can manipulate and draw upon. I know of no better system than these eight guides that I have adopted because they work for me. I've taught them to a great many other people for whom they worked just as well as for me.

GUIDES OF LOVE AND ROMANCE

Another set of twin guides are the guides of love and romance. I don't believe that anything worthwhile can be accomplished unless you romanticize whatever you're doing. If you don't put some romance into whatever you're doing, you don't get any fun out of it. And if there were no love in your heart, you wouldn't be a human being, because the main difference between the lower animals and the human being is that humans are capable of expressing the emotion of love. Love is a great builder of geniuses and of leaders; it's a great builder and maintainer of sound health. It's absolutely true without exception that to have the great capacity to love is to have the privilege of rubbing elbows with genius. The two guides of love and romance work to keep me friendly with what I'm doing and keep me young in body and mind. Believe me, they do just that. Not only do they keep me young in body and mind, they also keep me enthusiastic, sold on what I'm doing and without any drudgery in it. In other words, there's no such thing as hard work because I don't work at anything. I play at everything I do. Everything is a labor of love.

I recognize that before you get in a position where you can economically forget about earning a living, there's something that you have to think about that maybe takes a little of the pleasure out of work. But you can develop a system that'll make everything that you do a labor of love for the time being, whether you're washing dishes or digging ditches or anything else. When I go home, I help Annie Lou wash the dishes, not because she couldn't do it but because I want to feel that I'm not too good to help wash the dishes. And I get great joy out of doing it. I'm not above working in the garden either, because if I didn't do it, Annie Lou would do it while I'm gone and deprive me of the pleasure. It gives me a nice tan and good health. Learn to live the simple life, to be a human being instead of a stiff shirt or something else that you don't want to be (and nobody really wants to be). Learn to get love and romance into your life, and learn to have a system whereby that habit of love and romance will express itself in everything you do.

GUIDE FOR OVERALL WISDOM

The guide to overall wisdom is the comptroller of the other seven. His business is to keep them active, eternally engaged in your service. This guide adjusts you to every circumstance of your life, pleasant or unpleasant, so that you benefit by that circumstance. I can truthfully say that nothing comes to the mill of my life that isn't grist. I make grist out of everything. The more unpleasant things that come, the more grist I get out of them, because I doubly grind them to make sure they won't be anything else but grist.

Recognize that no experience in life is ever lost, whether it's good or bad. No experience is ever lost if you make the right adaptation of yourself to it. You can always profit by every experience in life if you have a system for doing it. Of course, if you let your emotions run wild and bring these unpleasant experiences into adulthood, you'll attract more unpleasant experiences than pleasant ones. But the peculiar thing about unpleasant circumstances is that they're cowardly. Get to where you will say, "Come on over here, little fellow. I've got a harness right here, and I'm going to put you to work." When they know you're going to put them to work, they find business around the corner, and they don't come your way so often.

If you fear unpleasant circumstances, they'll crowd down on you in flocks. They'll come in by the back door and the front door. They'll come when you're not expecting them or when you're unprepared to deal with them. I don't particularly invite unpleasant experiences, but if they are foolish enough to come my way, they'll find themselves ground up in my mill of life. Sure as anything, I'll make grist of them—but I'll not go down under them.

OBSTACLES TO POSITIVE THINKING

Eternal vigilance is the price one must pay to maintain a positive mental attitude, because of these unpleasant experiences and other natural opposites—the obstacles to positive thinking.

1: Tendency of the negative self to maneuver for power over you. There are entities working in your makeup all the time, constantly maneuvering to gain power over you on the negative side of life. You have to be on constant alert to see that those entities don't take you over.

2: Accumulated fears, doubts, and self-imposed limitations. You have to deal with them constantly lest they get the upper hand and become the dominating influence in your mind.

3: Negative influences, especially negative people. Negative influences include people who are negative, people that you work closely with, and people that you live with—maybe even some of your own relatives. If you aren't careful, you'll respond in kind and become as negative as they are. It may be necessary for you to live in the same house with somebody who's negative, but it's not necessary for you to be negative just because you're in the house with somebody who is. I'll admit, it can be a little bit difficult for you to immunize yourself against that kind of an influence, but you can do it. I have done it. Mahatma Gandhi did it. Look what he did with immunizing himself against things he didn't want.

4: Inborn negative traits. These are the traits you may have brought with you from birth. They can be transmuted into positive traits, once you ferret them out and find out what they are. I'm convinced that there are a lot of people who are born with natural traits of a negative nature. For instance, take a person who's born in an environment of poverty, where all of his relatives are poverty-stricken and all of the neighbors are poverty-stricken. From birth, he saw nothing but poverty, felt nothing but poverty, and heard nothing but poverty talk. That was the condition I was born in, and I know you can be born with that trait. One of the most difficult things that I had to do was to whip this inborn fear of poverty.

5: Worry over the lack of money and the lack of progress in your business, profession, or calling in life. You can either put in most of your time worrying over things, or you can transmute that state of mind into working out ways and means of overcoming those worries. Think about the positive side instead of the negative side. Worrying over the negative side is not going to do anything except to get you in deeper and deeper and deeper. That's all it's going to do.

6: Unrequited love and unbalanced emotional frustrations with the opposite sex. You don't have to let unrequited love affairs destroy your balance of mind, as so many people do. It's up to you to do something about it, to maintain a positive mental attitude, and to recognize that your first duty is to yourself. Get control of yourself and do not allow anybody, emotionally or otherwise, to upset your equilibrium. The Creator didn't intend that to be done, and you shouldn't let it be done either.

7: Unsound health, either real or imaginary. You can worry an awful lot about the things that you think might physically happen to you but never do. In the Materia Medica, we call it hypochondria—that's a two-and-a-half-dollar word with the doctors. Well, it used to be two and a half dollars but now it's five dollars, and sometimes a lot more than five dollars!

You can spend an awful lot of time becoming negative if you don't have a positive mental attitude toward your health, or if you don't develop and build up a health consciousness. Think in terms of health. Your mental attitude has a tremendous amount to do with what happens to your physical body. There's no doubt about it. Try it anytime. Have you ever had the experience when you're not feeling well, and some good piece of news comes along, how quickly you snap out of it? Maybe you weren't feeling so badly, but this good news did away with the feeling that you had.

8: Intolerance and lack of an open mind. These two things give some people a lot of trouble in maintaining a negative mental attitude.

9: Greed for more material possessions than you need. Once again, this is about the things that you accumulate, the price that you have to pay, the things that you have to conquer in order to have a positive mental attitude.

10: Lack of a definite major purpose.

11: Lack of a definite philosophy by which to live and guide your life. Did you know that the vast majority of people have no philosophy to live by? Without a philosophy, they live by hook or by crook, by chance, and by circumstance. They're like a dry leaf on the bosom of the wind, going whichever way the wind blows. There's nothing they can do about it because they have no philosophy of life. They have no set of rules to go by. Trusting to luck and to misfortune, misfortune generally rules. You have to have a philosophy that you can live by. There are many fine philosophies that you can die by, but I'm much more interested in one that you can live by, and that's what we're studying here.

This is a philosophy that you can live by in such a way that the neighbors around you look upon you as someone desirable. They feel happy to have you there and you feel happy to be there. You'll not only enjoy prosperity and contentment and peace of mind, but you'll reflect that to everybody that comes into contact with you. That's the way people should live. That's the kind of a mental attitude people should live by.

12: Letting others do your thinking for you. If you allow others to do your thinking, you'll never have a positive mental attitude because you won't have your own mind.

TWELVE GREAT AND ENDURING RICHES

Everyone desires to be rich, but not everyone knows what constitutes enduring riches. There are twelve great and enduring riches. I want you to familiarize yourself with them because before anybody can become rich, they must have a fairly well-balanced proportion of all of these twelve great riches. I want you to notice where I place money relative to its importance in regard to the others. It's number twelve, because there are eleven other things that are even more important than money if you're going to have a well-rounded-out, well-balanced life.

1. Positive mental attitude.
2. Sound physical health.

3. Harmony in human relations.
4. Freedom from fear.
5. Hope of future achievement.
6. Applied faith.
7. Willingness to share one's blessings.
8. To be engaged in a labor of love.
9. An open mind on all subjects. Tolerance toward all people.
10. Complete self-discipline.
11. The wisdom with which to understand people.
12. Money.

POINTS TO REMEMBER

1. Only efforts borne out of a positive mental attitude can be deemed worthy.
2. The five conditions of the mind that lead to a positive mental attitude.
3. You can never accomplish anything with a negative frame of mind.

3

THE BASIC ATTITUDE THAT BRINGS WEALTH AND PEACE OF MIND

A life of wealth enjoyed by a mind at peace comes most often to men who maintain a positive mental attitude. With definiteness of purpose you add great positive power to your own mental attitude, and you can use definite motives to sustain the actions which propel you toward your goal. At the same time you can set up spiritual guardians to keep your attitudes at a high "Yes" level, avoid conflicts of motive, tune-in on other positive minds.

The computers which are beginning to manage our world are complicated devices. Most of them, however, have a very simple basic principle: they say Yes or No. They either open a kind of electrical gate or they keep it closed, and by multiplying this process they can assimilate and select all kinds of information.

The mind of man is far more wonderful than any machine.

Within it, however, there seems to be a kind of Yes-No valve at the focal point of thinking. It is as though your awareness of a circumstance of life—sent to your brain by your sight, hearing and other senses—presents itself at the Yes-No point to be processed. A person who maintains a positive attitude will find every possible Yes in that circumstance and make it part of his life. A person who maintains a negative mental attitude will lean toward the No side, miss much that is good, live with much that is painful and damaging.

Nothing but a mental attitude? Nothing but a mental attitude, but it is right there that your success or your failure, your peace of mind or your nervous tension, your tendency toward good health or your tendency toward illness begins.

Fortunately it is possible for anyone to make the change from negativism to positivism, and thus basically condition his brain to bring all that is good in life. Moreover, there are certain "control levers" which the Creator makes available to us, and it is easy to see how successful people use these levers, once you know what they are.

I shall give you some here and some in other chapters so as to reinforce your memory. Now and then you will find repetition of names, facts and methods in this book, always with a view toward helping you remember.

Control your mental attitude with definiteness of purpose. Emerson said: "The world makes way for a man who knows where he is going."

Think what it means to know where you are going! Automatically you rid yourself of all kinds of fears and doubts which may have crept into the making-up-your-mind process. Your purpose is definite and—presto!—all the limitless forces of your mind focus upon that purpose and no other. Knowing your purpose, you cannot be led astray by circumstances or words which have nothing to do with your purpose. Where, before, a day's work may have contained a good deal of wasted motion, now your efforts are lined up so that each mental or physical motion helps every other motion.

You can see the connection with building wealth, for work done well is a basic wealth-builder. Now see the connection with peace of mind. A man who works wholeheartedly at his job is not concerned with such matters as finding fault with others, disturbing his conscience by cutting corners in his work, watching the clock and so forth. Nor will he be discouraged by any obstacles which may crop up; his positive and focused mental attitude keeps him in a prime position to handle problems and overcome them.

EFFICIENCY AND POSITIVITY

Is this a secret of "genius"? I have mentioned that many eminently successful men do not possess any greater intelligence than most other men possess. Yet their achievements are such that we may say that these men have "genius." Surely it is the positive mental attitude of these men which makes their brain-power, not greater, but more efficient and more available than most others'. When I spoke to such men as Henry Ford, Andrew Carnegie and Thomas A. Edison, I spoke with minds free of any fear or doubt that they could do anything they wished to do.

I know that Andrew Carnegie was well aware of the need for a positive mental attitude. Before he undertook to back me in my success, he really put me "on the spot" as to my mental attitude.

Looking at me shrewdly across his desk, that canny Scot said: "We've talked a long time and I have shown you the greatest opportunity a young man ever had to become famous, rich and useful. Now—if I choose you out of the two hundred and forty other applicants for this job—if I introduce you to the outstandingly successful men in America—if I help you get their collaboration in finding out the true philosophy of success—will you devote twenty years to the job, earning your own living as you go along? We have had sufficient discussion. I want your answer—yes or no."

I began to think of all the obstacles that would stand in my way. I began to think of all the hurdles I would have to jump. I began to think of all the time I would have to spend, and the big job of writing, and the problem of earning my living all that while—and so forth.

I spent twenty-nine seconds struggling with a negative mental attitude which, had it overcome me, would have affected me negatively ever after.

How do I know I took just twenty-nine seconds? Because, when I found the positive mental attitude which I had lost temporarily, and said "Yes!"—Mr. Carnegie showed me the stopwatch he had been holding beneath his desk. He had given me just one minute in which to show my positive state of mind otherwise, he felt, he would not have been able to depend on it. I had beaten the deadline by just thirty-one seconds, and thereby embraced an opportunity that was destined to change and improve the lives of millions of people, including my own.

A positive mind tunes in on other positive minds. Once I had accepted that great task and had set my mind confidently toward it, I found that my imagined obstacles simply melted away. Of course my positive mental attitude helped me not only in finding out the success secrets of some five hundred of America's wealthiest men, but also in making considerably more than a mere living. Am I a genius? I must say I have positive evidence I am not!

In meeting many men I discovered a very valuable fact: a positive mind automatically obtains benefit from other positive minds.

Are you aware of the general principle of radio broadcasting? It is this: when electrical vibrations of rapid frequency are impressed upon a wire, those vibrations leap into space. Another wire far away—the receiving antenna—can pick them up, and thus a message or a picture is transmitted over thousands of miles, or millions of miles in space-age communication.

There are electrical currents in the brain. They give you a private broadcasting station through which you may send out any kind of thought vibrations you desire. Keep that station busy sending out thoughts of a positive nature, thoughts which will benefit others, and you will find you can receive kindred thought vibrations from other minds whose attitude is tuned to yours.

When I visited such successful men as those I have mentioned, and many others such as John Wanamaker, Frank A. Vanderlip, Edward Bok and Woodrow Wilson, both they and I felt the attunement of mind to mind. Otherwise I surely would have met with opposition when I asked those top-ranking men to give me of their time and experience. Not only did such men spend hours talking to me, but also they served as my teachers and guides for year after year, and charged me nothing.

Believe in what you are doing, and you too will see the great effect of your belief upon those whom you may request to help you. Doubt yourself and the No part of your mind takes over and draws defeat instead of victory.

This barely sketches in the all-pervasive power of a positive mental attitude. Let us look at some of the other "control levers" which combine with a positive mental attitude to give you wealth and peace of mind for an entire, victorious lifetime.

THE NINE MAJOR MOTIVES

It is not for nothing that court trials often concern themselves with questions of motive. Everything you do is the result of one or more motives. In various combinations we use nine basic motives. The seven positive motives are:

1. The emotion of LOVE
2. The emotion of SEX
3. The desire for MATERIAL GAIN
4. The desire for SELF-PRESERVATION
5. The desire for FREEDOM OF BODY AND MIND
6. The desire for SELF-EXPRESSION
7. The desire for PERPETUATION OF LIFE AFTER DEATH

The two negative emotions are:

1. The emotion of ANGER AND REVENGE
2. The emotion of FEAR

In those nine motives you can find the roots of everything you do or refrain from doing. Peace of mind is attained only by the exercise of the seven positive motives as a general pattern of life. Rarely if ever does a person who has peace of mind exercise the two negative motives or emotions. You cannot have peace of mind while you fear anything or anyone. You cannot have peace of mind while you entertain the kind of anger which brings you to a desire for revenge or a desire to injure another, no matter what the justification may seem to be.

THE PRICE OF PEACE OF MIND

Great men have no time to waste with a desire to injure others. If they did, they would not be great men. Great men are not immune to fear, but theirs is not the kind of fear that hangs on constantly and takes over all of life. Look to small, mean men to see lifelong patterns of fear and anger. Their minds are so filled with these negative influences that they cannot find the power to shape the circumstances they desire.

Recently I heard about a man, now seventy, who fifteen years ago lost all his money in a real estate venture. Taking the advice of a friend, he had borrowed heavily in order to invest in vacant swampland on the assumption that in a couple of years the land would be in great demand for building lots. This did not transpire, the man's notes became due, and he had to see his retail shoe business sold out from under him.

The friend who had badly advised him also had lost money. Nevertheless this man became filled with hatred toward his friend and said he would get even "if it's the last thing I do." It nearly was. Five years of hatred left him incapable even of doing business. Meanwhile the friend prospered and seemed far out of reach of any puny revenge. The man who had lost his money at length lost the balance wheel of his mind and had to spend six months in a quiet place in the country surrounded by a high wall.

In his last month of confinement, however, he was sufficiently recovered to listen to an adviser who pointed out to him that hatred and the desire for revenge had done him far more harm than had been done by his losing his money. He was persuaded to forgive the friend who had led him into the real estate deal. He even wrote to this man, telling of his change of heart.

When he went back into business it was with love of his fellow men and the determination to keep his mind filled with positive, constructive motives. Beginning at the age of sixty, he built a new career. Now, at seventy, he is fairly well off, and most of all he has peace of mind, the one form of wealth which is indispensable.

I myself have suffered from the effects of negative motives from time to time. When I went into hiding, as discussed in the last chapter, I acted at first upon a very wise motive of self-preservation. Soon, however, this turned into fear and with the fear came misery. Fortunately I saw in time what was happening to me. It cannot happen again.

You can call upon Ten Princes of Guidance to stand at the doors of your mind. You can make yourself aware of certain principles of personal guidance and guardianship; and to make these principles real and memorable, you can personalize them— see them as so many Princes in armor who stand at the doors of your mind. These Princes challenge every thought-vibration which seeks to enter. They keep your mind positive, effective and free of discord. I shall name my own Princes, a list which you may wish to modify to suit your own life-requirements.

The Prince of Peace of Mind. He stands at the very outer door and asks all callers if they come in peace to share my peace. If not, they are turned away.

The Prince of Hope and Faith. He admits only those influences which keep my mind alerted with belief in my mission in life.

The Prince of Love and Romance. He brings into my mind only those influences which keep love eternally fresh in my heart.

The Prince of Sound Physical Health. He knows the kind of mental influences which can destroy health, and admits only those states of mind which help the body maintain its vigor.

The Prince of Financial Security. When I desire him to stand on guard, he admits no thoughts save those which bring me worthy financial benefit.

The Prince of Overall Wisdom. He is charged with passing certain thoughts into my store of knowledge when he sees they will benefit me or help me benefit others.

The Prince of Patience. He keeps away all impulses to rush, to tackle jobs half-prepared, to be in any way impatient with the power of time.

The Prince of Normhill. "Normhill" is a very personal word I have created for my own use. Combining certain names, it means to me what it cannot mean to any other. Just so, create your own name for your own very personal Prince. This Prince stands guard along with all the others. The others from time to time may be relieved of duty; for instance, one hardly may wish continually to keep out all thoughts except those which have to do with financial security. Your special personal Prince is always there, representing all the special personal influences in your life. Normhill is my ambassador-at-large who performs services not assigned to the other members of my invisible family of guides.

When you have made yourself well aware of your corps of spiritual Princes, they serve to rally all your forces to solve any problem or to set up special lines of defense.

Sometimes I find myself talking to someone whose antagonistic attitude begins to invade my peace of mind. Very well—I send a special alert to the Prince of Peace of Mind. Immediately he takes charge of the ramparts with doubled strength, and I am calm and in control of my own mind once more.

Or, let us say, I feel some physical ache or pain. I call upon the Prince of Sound Physical Health to look into the cause, and I get good results. I believe I have received benefits of healing which are beyond the power of ordinary medical science to explain.

My Princes of Guidance receive a certain compensation for their services. Their "pay" is my eternal gratitude. Daily I express this gratitude, first to each of the Princes individually, then to all of them in their mighty group. You will find this expression of gratitude of great help in keeping your mind alerted to its own powers. I know that if I ever neglect it, I feel a neglect on the part of my Princes. When, once again, I make myself aware every day that I have great spiritual forces at my command—there they are once more, as strong as ever.

Don't let the motive of material gain conflict with the motive of freedom. Freedom of body is easy to see and understand; but freedom of mind is a subtle matter. Fear and anger put the mind behind bars. Guilt wraps the mind in chains. To add a bit of levity to a serious matter: Once there was a man who was encouraged to know himself. Immediately he handcuffed himself to his bed, so he would not get up and rifle his own pockets during the night.

All too often the motive of material gain—excellent in itself—conflicts with the excellent motive of freedom of body and mind because in gaining what is material we give up freedom of mind; we load the mind with guilt and fear because we do not act honestly.

In addition, one who makes his money through taking dishonest advantage of his fellow men has cheated himself of the genuine joy which comes with honest success. When you obey the rules of a game, and win, you have done something for your soul. When you cheat and win, you only call it winning, but you have really lost instead.

I believe I was fortunate in starting my career very early in life, so that I learned life's lessons quite early. Let me tell you of an experience I had while I was holding my first job. I was just out of business college and I was inexperienced in the ways of life and the character of men.

My employer owned a number of banks. He had placed his son as a cashier of one of his banks, in a distant town. One night a hotel manager in that town telephoned me, saying my employer's son was in serious difficulty. He had not been able to reach my employer. Immediately, I boarded the train and arrived in the town early the next morning.

When I went to the bank I found the door closed but unlocked. Inside, I discovered that the vault had been left open and beautiful green currency was scattered all over the teller's counter.

I closed the door and picked up the telephone. I managed to get my employer on the phone and told him why I had gone to that town and what I had found on my arrival. In great distress, he said: "Go ahead and count the money. Balance the books. Draw a draft on me for whatever shortage there may be."

I settled down to counting the money. To my great surprise, not a cent was missing.

I sat there looking at those piles of greenbacks. My youth had been tragic, turbulent and poor. My present state was one of bare solvency. I sat there looking at nearly $50,000 in cash, knowing that I could put at least half of it into my pocket and nobody would be the wiser. My employer's son showed obvious signs of mental instability. Everyone would assume he had taken the money. He even had acted as though he had filled his own pockets—and I was the only one who knew he had not.

The motive of material gain nudged heavily at me. But the motive of freedom said: Don't do it. Or rather, it was "something" that kept me honest, for at that time I could not have named the major motives. Perhaps that "something" was the result of certain sessions I had had with my stepmother before I had left home, in which she had instilled into me the fact that I was in control of my own mind and that always I must live with myself.

I locked the money into the vault forthwith, then phoned my employer and told him there was no deficiency to make up; not a cent had been stolen. I walked out of that bank with a mind at peace, a mind that was free and joyously positive.

Forever after I have placed the motive of freedom ahead of the motive of material gain. I have succeeded in having all the money I need without ever hampering either my inward or outward freedom.

LIFE IS A MIRROR

This episode was one of several which led me straight to Andrew Carnegie and my realization of my goal in life. My employer was grateful for the way in which I had protected his son's reputation as best I could. He was responsible later for my entering Georgetown University Law School. This led through a chain of circumstances to my assignment to interview Mr. Carnegie. If I had yielded to the material gain motive that day in the bank, the Science of Personal Achievement might never have come into being.

Yes, as Emerson suggested, there is a silent partner in all our transactions, and woe is the lot of the man who tries to drive a sharp bargain with Life.

Life reflects your own thoughts back to you. Thoughts are things, a poet said, and truly they have an existence of their own, so that a curse comes back to curse you and a blessing comes back to bless you, reflected by the mighty mirror of life. Another poet said: "I am the master of my fate, I am the captain of my soul." This too is true, and the two truths harmonize. Send out positive thoughts from a positively oriented soul and the world will reflect back greater and greater positive influences to help you.

Turn back and read the list of nine basic motives. Concentrate on the seven positive motives. Remember it is possible for these motives to come into conflict, as we have seen; but by and large they drive one way, and with a positive mental attitude they take you the way you want to go. We shall not say farewell to the motives till we are finished with this book; but let us now pay our respects briefly.

Love has limitless scope. Handle it in a spirit of reverence, for it is tuned to the Eternal. Give freely of it and you will attract as much as or more than you give; stop giving love and you stop receiving. With no other emotion or motive or desire is the mirror of life so very evident.

Sex is the great creative force of the universe. On its highest plane it merges with love; but love can exist without being sexual. The mighty power of sex can be transmuted into action for the achievement of profound purpose. On the other hand, sex may be debauched and misused, and it is in this guise that it brings grief and trouble to mankind and gives itself an underserved bad reputation.

Self-preservation can become a negative force when one seeks it without regard to the rights of other people. It is instilled by Nature to help us stay alive. Even so, the human being assumes the prerogative of rising above it. When a ship is sinking it is women and children first, and there are many parallel instances which call forth a nobility in human nature.

Self-expression is part of finding one's self. It is part of one's freedom to be one's self. Thus it is positive, constructive and infinitely valuable. Only make sure that your own means of self-expression do not demean or damage others.

Perpetuation of life after death belongs among the earliest

beliefs and motives of mankind. It should be bounded by common sense and a true understanding of one's relationship to that change known as death. When wrapped in superstition and fear, this motive leads only to wretchedness. It can turn life into a preparation for death and hamper an entire civilization.

The surest way of finding peace of mind. The surest way of finding peace of mind is that which helps the greatest number of others to find it.

Let this be your guide to your use of the great motivating forces; then you will know you are using them correctly, not corrupting them.

Is there peace of mind in prayer? There can be. There should be. But note how many people go to prayer only in the hour of a misfortune, when the motive of fear dominates their minds. The approach must be negative in that case, and so, in terms of peace of mind, the results must be negative as well.

Prayers which bring peace of mind proceed from a mind which gives forth a confident message even though that mind may be afflicted with problems and sorrow. Prayers which free great forces to solve problems are born in minds which know that the problems can be solved once the forces are found—and have perfect confidence in the existence of those forces.

Along with many others I see evidence of an Intelligence beyond man's. I believe that the positively conditioned mind may at times tune in on that Intelligence. Yet mind-conditioning through prayer or resolution is something an individual must accomplish for himself. When the Creator made man free to seek his own destiny, and choose between good and evil, he gave man this prerogative as well. Every great accomplishment of any man at any time first had to exist as a thought before it could exist as reality.

Have you recognized the Supreme Secret?

POINTS TO REMEMBER

1. A life of wealth is only enjoyed by someone who possesses a positive mental attitude.
2. Control your mental attitude with definiteness of purpose.
3. The nine basic motives for any human endeavor.

4

GOING THE EXTRA MILE

Going the extra mile means rendering of more service and better service than you're paid to render, doing it all the time, and doing it with a pleasant, pleasing mental attitude.

One of the reasons why there are so many failures in the world is that the majority of people do not even go the first mile, let along the second one. If they do go the first mile, they usually gripe as they go along and make themselves a darned nuisance to people around them. I suppose you know the type. But it doesn't apply to any of you, because if you were like that before you got into this philosophy, you're going to get over it very fast.

I don't know of any one quality or trait that can get a person an opportunity quicker than to go out of his or her way to do somebody a favor, or do something useful. It's the one thing you can do in life without having to ask anybody for the privilege of doing it. Unless you form the habit of going the extra mile and make yourself as indispensable as you possibly can, the only other way you'll ever be free, and independent, and self-determining, and financially independent in old age will be by a stroke of good luck, a rich uncle or rich aunt dying, or something of that sort. I don't know of any way anybody can make himself or herself indispensable *except* by going the extra mile, by rendering some sort of service that you're not expected to render, and rendering it in the right sort of a mental attitude.

Mental attitude is important. If you gripe about going the extra mile, chances are that it won't bring you very many returns. Where do you suppose I get my authority for emphasizing this principle of going the extra mile? Experience.

I've watched the way nature does things, because you won't go wrong if you follow the way or the habits of nature. Conversely, if you fail to recognize and follow the way nature does things, you'll get into trouble sooner or later—it's just a question of time. There is an overall plan in which this universe operates, no matter what you call the first cause of that plan, or the operator of it, or the creator of it. There's just one set of natural laws, and it's up to every individual to discover them and adjust himself favorably to them. Above all, nature requests and demands that every living thing go the extra mile in order to eat, in order to live, and in order to survive. Man wouldn't survive one season if it were not for this law of going the extra mile.

Don't render a million dollars' worth of service today and expect to get a bank check for it tomorrow. If you start out to render a million dollars' worth of service, you might have to render it a little bit at a time. You're going to have to get yourself recognized for doing it and you'll have to go the extra mile for a little while before anybody takes notice of you. However, be careful not to go the extra mile *too* long without somebody taking notice of you. If the right fellow doesn't take notice, look around until you find the right fellow who will. In other words, if your present employer doesn't recognize you, fire the employer sooner or later and let his competitor know what kind of service you're rendering. I assure you it won't hurt your chances a bit. Have a little competition as you go along.

Nobody ever accepts a rule or does anything without a motive, and I have a great variety of reasons why you should go the extra mile.

THE LAW OF INCREASING RETURNS

The law of increasing returns means that you'll get back more than you give out, whether it's good or bad, whether it's positive or negative. That's the way the law of nature works. **Whatever you give out, whatever you do to or for another person, or whatever you give out from yourself, comes back to you greatly multiplied in kind.** No exception whatsoever. It doesn't always come back very quickly; sometimes it takes longer than you expect. But you may be sure that if you send out some negative influence, it's going to come back to you sooner or later. You may not recognize what caused it, but it'll come back. It won't overlook you.

The law of increasing returns is eternal, automatic, and it's working all the time. It's just as inexorable as the law of gravitation. Nobody in the world can circumvent it, go around it, or have it suspended for one moment. It's operating all the time. The law of increasing returns means that when you go out of your way to render more service and better service than you're paid to render, it's impossible for you *not* to get back more than you really did, because the law of increasing returns takes care of that. If you're working for a salary, the law takes care of it in additional wages, greater responsibilities, promotions, or opportunities to go into business for yourself. In a thousand and one different ways, it'll come back.

THE LAW OF COMPENSATION

It doesn't always come back from the source to which you rendered the service. Don't be afraid to render service to a greedy buyer or a greedy employer. It makes no difference to whom you render service. If you render it in good faith and in good spirit, and keep doing it as a matter of habit, it's equally impossible for you *not* to be compensated as it is to *be* compensated. Therefore, you don't have to be too careful about the person to whom you render it. In fact, apply this principle with *everybody*, no matter who it is—strangers, acquaintances, business associates, and relatives, too. Make it your business to render useful service to everyone, regardless of the shape, form, or fashion in which you touch them.

The only way you can increase the space that you occupy in the world—and I don't mean just the physical space, but also the mental and the spiritual space as well—will be determined by the quality and the quantity of the service that you render. In addition to the quality and the quantity, is the mental attitude in which you render it. Those are the determining factors as to how far you'll go in life, how much you'll get out of life, how much you'll enjoy life, and how much peace of mind you'll have.

SELF-PROMOTION

Self-promotion elicits the favorable attention of other people. If you're alert-minded and take notice, you'll find in any organization those people that are going the extra mile. You'll find out very quickly. And if you watch the procedure and the records of those people who are going the extra mile, you'll see that when there are promotions around, they're the ones that get them. They don't have to ask for them; it's not necessary at all. Employers *look* for people who will go the extra mile. It permits one to become indispensable in many different human relationships. It enables one to command more than the average compensation.

GIVING FEEDS THE SOUL

I want you to know that it also does something to your soul inside of you; it makes you feel better. And if there were no other reason in the world why you should go the extra mile, I'd say that would be adequate. There are a lot of things in life that cause us to have negative feelings or cause us unpleasant experiences and feelings. However, this is one thing that you can do for yourself that'll *always* give you a pleasant feeling. And if you'll go back through your own experiences, I'm sure you'll remember that you never did a kind thing for anybody without getting a great deal of joy out of it. Maybe the other fellow didn't appreciate it, but that's unimportant.

It's like love. To have loved, that alone is a great privilege. It makes no difference whatsoever whether your love was returned by the other person. You've had the benefit by the emotion of love itself. So it is by the principle of going the extra mile. It'll do something *to you*. It'll give you greater courage. It'll enable you to overcome inhibitions and inferiority complexes that you've been storing through the years. There is so much benefit available to stepping out and making yourself useful to somebody.

If you do something courteous or useful for somebody who

is not expecting it, don't be too surprised when they look at you in a quizzical sort of way, as much as to say, "Well, I just wonder why you're doing that." Some people will be a little bit surprised when you go out of your way to be useful to them.

MENTAL AND PHYSICAL BENEFITS

Going the extra mile in all forms of service will lead to mental growth and physical perfection across all areas as well as greater ability and skill in one's chosen vocation. Whether you're delivering a lecture or making up your notebook, or filling your job, if it's something that you're going to do over and over again in your life, make up your mind that every time you do it, you will excel beyond all previous efforts on your part. In other words, become a constant challenge to yourself. See how quickly and how rapidly you will grow if you'll go at it in that way.

I have never delivered a lecture in my life that I didn't intend to deliver better than I did previously. I don't always do it, but that's my intention. It makes no difference what kind of an audience I have, whether I have a big class or a small class. I don't often have small classes, but when I do, I put just as much into a small class as a big one, not only because I want to be useful to my students, but because I want to grow and I want to develop. Out of effort, out of struggle, and out of the use of your faculties comes growth. It enables one to profit by the law of contrast. You won't have to advertise that one very much—it'll advertise itself—because the majority of people around you are *not* going to be going the extra mile, and that's all the better for you.

If everybody went the extra mile this would be a grand world to live in, but you wouldn't be able to cash in on this principle as definitely as you can now because you'd have a tremendous amount of competition. Don't worry. I can assure you you're not going to have it. You'll be in a class by yourself. There will be cases where people you work with or are associated with will be shown up for *not* going the first mile, let alone the second one, and they won't like that. Are you going to cry about that one and quit and go back to your old habits, just because the other fellow doesn't like what you're doing? Of course not.

It's your individual responsibility to succeed. That's your sole responsibility. You can't afford to let anybody's ideas, idiosyncrasies, or notions get in the way of your success. You can't afford to do that. You should be fair with other people, but beyond that, you're under no obligations to let anybody's opinions or ideas stop you from being successful. I'd like to see the person that could stop me from being successful. I'd love to see what he looks like, and I want you to feel that way about it, too. I want you to make up your mind that you're going to put these laws into operation and that you're not going to let anybody stop you from doing it. It leads to the development of a positive, pleasing mental attitude, which is among the more important traits of a pleasing personality —actually, not *among* the more important; it *is* the most important one. A positive mental attitude is the first trait of a pleasing personality.

It's a marvelous thing to know what you can do to change the chemistry of your brain so that you're positive instead of negative. Do you know how easy it is? It's as easy as getting in that frame of mind where you want to do something useful for the other fellow, without rendering service on the one hand and picking his pocket with the other. You're doing it just because of the goodness that you get *out* of doing it. You know that if you render more service and better service than you're paid to render, sooner or later you'll be paid for more than you do and you'll be paid willingly. That's the way the law works. That's the law of compensation. It's an eternal law, it never forgets, and it has a perfectly marvelous bookkeeping system. You may be sure that when you are giving out the right kind of service with the right kind of a mental attitude, you are piling up credits that'll come back to you multiplied, sooner or later.

UNLIMITED BENEFITS

Going the extra mile tends to develop a keen, alert imagination because it is a habit that keeps you continuously seeking new and more efficient ways of rendering useful service. The reason that's important is that, as you begin to look around to see how many places, and ways, and means there are in helping the other fellow to find *himself*, you find *yourself*.

One of the most outstanding things that I discovered in my research was that when you have a problem or an unpleasant situation you don't know how to solve, when you've done everything you know, and when you've tried every source you know of, and you're still at a stalemate, there is always one thing that you can do. I want to tell you that if you'll do that one thing, the chances are that you not only will solve your problem, but you'll also learn a great lesson. That one thing is to find somebody who has an equal or a greater problem and start where you stand, then and there, to help that *other* person. Lo and behold, it unlocks something in you. It unlocks cells of the brain, unlocking cells that permit Infinite Intelligence to come into your brain and give you the answer to the solution of your problem.

I don't know why that works, but do you know how I know that it *does* work? Do you know why I can make that statement so positive and not qualify it? I arrived at that decision by experience, by trying it out hundreds and hundreds of times myself, and by seeing it tried out hundreds and hundreds of times by my students to whom I have recommended that same thing. What a simple thing that is! I don't know *what it does* and I don't know *why it works*. There are a lot of things in life I don't know and there are a lot of things you don't know. There are also some things that you do know that you don't do much about. This is one of those things that I don't know anything about but I do something about.

I follow the law because I know that if I need my own mind to be opened up to receive opportunity, the best way in the world to open it up is to start looking around to see how many other people I can help.

PERSONAL INITIATIVE

Personal initiative gets you into the habit of looking around for something useful to do and going out and doing it without somebody telling you to do it. That old man Procrastination is a sour old bird and he causes a lot of trouble in this world. People put off things until the day after tomorrow that they should have done the day before yesterday. Every one of us is guilty of it. I know I'm not free of it and I know you're not, either. But I can tell you I'm freer of it than I was a few years back. I can find a lot of things to do now and I find them because I get joy out of doing them. Anytime you're going the extra mile, you're going to get joy out of what you're doing; otherwise, you won't go the extra mile. It will help you develop the quality of personal initiative and help you overcome the quality of procrastination.

Going the extra mile also serves to build the confidence of others on one's integrity and general ability, and it aids one in mastering the destructive habit of procrastination. It develops definiteness of purpose, without which one cannot hope for success. That alone would be enough to justify it. It gives you an objective, so that you don't go around and around in circles like a goldfish in a bowl, always coming back to where you started with something that you didn't start out with. Definiteness of purpose comes out of this business of going the extra mile. It also enables you to make your work a joy instead of a burden—you get to where you love it. If you're not engaged in a labor of love, you're wasting a lot of your time.

One of the greatest joys in the world is being permitted to engage in the thing that you would rather do than all other things. When you're going the extra mile, you're doing just exactly that. You don't have to do it, nobody expects you to do it, and nobody asks you to do it. Certainly no employer would ask his employees to go the extra mile. He might ask for extra help once in a while, but he wouldn't do it as a regular thing. It's something that you do on your own initiative, and it gives a dignity to your labor. Even if you're digging a ditch, you're *helping* somebody, and there's a certain dignity to that which takes the fatigue and the unpleasantness out of the labor.

Going the extra mile often gives the greatest amount of joy. You might think you go the extra mile being married, but what about before you get married? Believe me, I spent a lot of time burning midnight oil and I didn't consider it hard work at all. It was my own idea and I used my initiative, but I also got a lot of joy out of doing it and I made it pay off. When you're courting the girl of your choice (or being courted by the man of your choice), it's marvelous how much sleep you can lose and still not be seriously hurt by it. Wouldn't it be a wonderful thing if you could put the same attitude into your relations with people professionally or in the business that you put into courtship? We're going to start sparking again.

It's going to start at home, with our own mates. I couldn't begin to tell you the number of married couples that I've started in on a new sparking spree. They're getting a lot of joy out of it. It saves a lot of friction and a lot of argument. It cuts down expenses. Go ahead and laugh, but it will do you good.

I don't mean to be facetious. I'm very serious when I say that there is one of the finest places in the world to start going the extra mile. When you start going the extra mile with somebody that you haven't seen, sit down and have a little sales talk with them. Tell them that you've changed your attitude and you want a mutual agreement for both parties to change the attitude so that from here on out, *all* of us are going the extra mile. We're going to relate together on a different basis, where we'll all get joy out of it, more peace of mind, and more happiness in living. Wouldn't it be a wonderful thing if you went home tonight and had that kind of speech with your mate? It wouldn't hurt; it might help. Your mate might not be impressed by it, but you will be. Nothing will hinder you from enjoying it.

What about that person in business that you haven't been getting along so well with? Why not go in tomorrow morning with a smile and walk over to him or her and shake his hand and say, "Now look here and listen up, pal. From here on out, let's you and I enjoy working together." What would he say? It wouldn't work, huh? Oh, yes, it would. You try it and see. There's another thing that we have called pride, and if there's one thing that does more damage in this world than any other one, it's that little thing called pride. Don't be afraid. Don't be afraid to humiliate yourself if it's going to build better human relations with the people that you have to associate with all the time.

ESTABLISH OBLIGATION

Going the extra mile is the only thing that gives one the right to ask for promotions or more pay. Did you ever stop to think about that? You don't have a leg to stand on if you go to the purchaser of your services and ask for more money or for promotion to a better job unless, for some time previously, you have been going the extra mile and doing more than you're paid for. Obviously, if you're doing no more than you're paid for, then you're being paid for all you're entitled to, aren't you? Certainly, you are. So you have to first start going the extra mile and put the other fellow under obligation to you before you can ask any favors of him. And if you have enough people whom you have put under obligations to you by going the extra mile, when you need some favor, you can always turn in one direction or other and get it. It's a nice thing to know that you have that kind of credit hanging around, isn't it? I want you to have that kind of credit with other people and I want to teach you the technique by which you can do that.

NATURE GOES THE EXTRA MILE

We get our cue as to the soundness of the principle of going the extra mile by observing nature, and there's quite a bit of illustration regarding that. You will see that nature goes the extra mile by producing not only enough of everything for her needs but also a surplus for emergencies and waste. It shows this by the blooms on the trees and the fishes in the seas. She doesn't just produce enough fish to perpetuate the species; she produces enough to feed the snakes and the alligators and everything else. She produces those that die of natural causes, and even more, so there's enough to perpetuate the species. Nature is most bountiful in her business of going the extra mile, and in return, she is very demanding in seeing that every living creature goes the extra mile. Bees are provided with honey as compensation for their services in fertilizing the flowers in which the honey is attractively stored.

But they have to perform the service to get the honey, and it must be performed in advance.

You've heard it said that the birds of the air and the beasts of the jungle neither weave nor spin, but they always live and eat. If you observe wildlife at all, you'll see they don't eat without performing some sort of service, without working or doing something before they can eat. Take a flock of common old cornfield crows, for instance. They have to be organized in order to travel in flocks. And they have sentinels to protect them and codes by which they warn one another. In other words, they have to do a lot of educating before they can even eat safely.

Nature requires man to go the extra mile if he's going to have food. All food comes out of the ground, and if he's going to have food, he's got to plant seed. He can't live entirely on what nature plants (at least not in civilized life). On islands where they're not civilized, I suppose they depend on eating raw coconuts and what have you, but in civilized life, we have to plant our food in the ground. We have to clear the ground first before we plow it, harrow it, fence it, protect it against predatory animals and so forth. All of that costs labor and time and money. All of that has to be done in advance or you're not going to eat. I wouldn't have any trouble at all selling this idea that nature makes everybody go the extra mile to a farmer, because he already knows it beyond any question of a doubt. He knows every minute of his life that if he doesn't go the extra mile, he doesn't eat and he doesn't have anything to sell. A new employee can't start going the extra mile and immediately demand top wages or the best job in the place. It doesn't work out that way. You have to establish a record, a reputation. You have to get yourself recognized and received before you can begin to put the pressure on to get compensation back. If you go the extra mile in the right sort of mental attitude, chances are a thousand to one you'll never have to ask for compensation for the service you render, because it'll be tendered to you automatically, in the way of promotions or increased salary.

LAW OF COMPENSATION

Throughout the whole universe, everything has been so arranged through the law of compensation (and so adequately described by Emerson) that nature's budget is balanced. Everything has its opposite equivalent in something else. Positive and negative in every unit of energy, day and night, hot and cold, success and failure, sweet and sour, happiness and misery, man and woman. Everywhere and in everything, one may see the law of action and reaction in operation. Everything you do, everything you think, and every thought that you release causes a reaction, on somebody else or on you as the person releasing the thought. Because when you release a thought, you're not through with it. Every thought that you express, silently even, becomes a definite part of the pattern of your subconscious mind.

If you store in that subconscious mind enough negative thoughts, you'll be predominantly negative. And if you follow the habit of releasing only the positive thoughts, your subconscious pattern will be predominantly positive, and you will attract to you all of the things that you want. If you're negative, you'll repel the things that you want and attract only the things you don't want. That's a law of nature, too. Going the extra mile is one of the finest ways that I know to educate your subconscious mind to attract to you the things you want and to repel the things you don't want.

It's an established fact that if you neglect to develop and apply this principle of going the extra mile, you will never become personally successful, and you will never become financially independent. I know it's sound because I've had a great privilege that you haven't had yet, but you will have, in time. I've had the privilege of observing a great many thousands of people, some of whom applied the principle of going the extra mile and some of whom did not. I've had the privilege of finding out what happened to those who did and those who didn't. **And I know beyond any question of a doubt that nobody ever rises above the ordinary stations in life or mediocrity without the habit of going the extra mile.** It just doesn't happen. If I had discovered one case, just one case where somebody went on to the top without going the extra mile, I would say then that there are exceptions, but I am in a position to say there are no exceptions because I have never found that one case. I can definitely tell you from my own experiences that I have never had a major benefit of any kind in the world that I didn't get as the result of going the extra mile.

I want you to become self-determining, so you can do these things without the help of anybody. The payoff will come to you when you can go out and do anything in this world that you want to do, and regardless of whether anybody wants you to do it or whether they want to help you or whether they don't, you can do it on your own. That's one of the grandest, most glorious feelings that I know—that whatever I want to do, I can do it. I don't have to ask anybody, not even my wife. But if I had to ask her, I would, because I'm on good terms with her.

PEACE OF MIND

Here's a little item now that's not to be sniffed at: peace of mind that I got out of all those twenty years of going the extra mile. Do you have any idea how many people there are in the world at any one time who are willing to do anything for twenty years in succession without getting something back out of it? Do you have any idea how many people there are in this world who are willing to do something for only three days in succession without being sure they're going to get something out of it? You'd be surprised at how few there are.

We're looking at one of the grandest opportunities that a human being could possibly have, especially here in this country where we really can create our own destiny and where we can express ourselves any way we want. Speech is free, activities are free, and education is free. There's wonderful opportunity to go the extra mile in any direction you want to travel in life. And yet, most people are not doing it. I have seen a time when there were not so many people interested in the philosophy because they were prosperous. They were doing all right and they had no troubles to speak of. Today, almost everybody has troubles, or they think they do.

Do you know what I do instead of finding out what's wrong with the rest of the world? Do you know how I put in my time? I try to find out what I can do to correct this guy here. I have to eat with him, sleep with him, shave his face every morning, wash his face, and give him a bath now and then. You have no idea how many things I have to do for him! I have to live with the guy, twenty-four hours a day.

I put in my time trying to improve myself, and, through myself, I try to improve my friends and my students, by writing books, by delivering lectures, and by teaching in other ways.

It pays off very much better than it would if I sat down and took the old newspapers and read all of the murder stories and all of the divorce scandals and everything that's blazoned across the pages every day. I'm still talking about this fellow Napoleon Hill, who didn't have sense enough to decline Andrew Carnegie's offer to work twenty years for nothing. His declining years will be years of happiness because of the seeds of kindness and help he has sown in the hearts of others.

If I had my life to live over again, I'd live it just exactly the way I have. I'd make all the mistakes I made. I'd make them at the time in life when I made them, early on so I'd have time enough to correct some of them. And that period during which I would come into peace of mind and understanding would be in the afternoon of life, not in the forenoon, because I couldn't take it. When you're young, you can take it. But when you pass the noon hour and you go into the afternoon, your energies are not as great as they were before. Your physical energy, and sometimes your mental capacity, is not as great. You can't take as much trouble as you can in your days of youth. And you haven't got so many years left to correct the mistakes that you made.

To have the tranquility and the peace of mind that I have today, in the afternoon of life, is one of the great joys that has come out of this philosophy. If you ask me what has been my greatest compensation, I would say that's it. There are so many people at my age, and even much younger than I, who haven't found peace of mind and never will. They never will, because they're looking for it in the wrong place. They're not doing anything about it; they're expecting somebody else to do something about it for them. Peace of mind is something that you've got to get for yourself. First of all, you've got to earn it. As to how anybody can get peace of mind, a few of you would be surprised where you have to really start looking for it. It's not where the average person is looking for it. It's not out there in the joys of what money will buy or out there in the joys of recognition and fame and fortune. You'll find peace of mind in the humility of the one individual's own heart.

Engage in at least one act of going the extra mile every day. You can choose your own circumstance, even if it's nothing more than telephoning an acquaintance and wishing him good fortune. You'll be surprised what'll happen to you when you begin to call up your friends that you have been neglecting for some time and just say, "You were on my mind. I was thinking about you, and I just wanted to call and say how do you do, and I hope you are feeling as good as I am." You'd be surprised at what that'll do to you and what it'll do to your friend, too. It doesn't have to be a close personal friend. It just has to be somebody you know. Or, maybe relieve a friend from duty for half an hour or so, or have a neighbor send over his children while he attends the movies, or do a little babysitting for one of your neighbors. If you're going to be at home anyway, with children of your own, maybe you know a neighbor who would like to get off and go down to the movies but can't get away from her children. The children may be noisy, and they'll probably fight with your children, but if you're a real diplomat, you'll keep them apart. She'll be under obligation to you, and you'll feel that you've really been kind by helping out somebody who otherwise wouldn't have had a little freedom. It'd be a nice thing for some of you people who don't have any children to say, "Why don't I come over and baby-sit for you while you go out? You and your husband can go on a little courtship. Let me come over and babysit for you while you go out to the movie or go to a show." You'll have to know your neighbors pretty well in order to do that. Certainly, most of you would have some neighbor that you could approach on some such basis, and they wouldn't think you were crazy.

It's not so much what you do to the other fellow. It's what you do to yourself by finding ways and means of going the extra mile in little ways. Did you know that both the successes in life as well as the failures are made up of little things? So little that they're often overlooked, because the things that make success are such small and seemingly insignificant things.

I know people who are so popular they couldn't have an enemy. One of them is my distinguished business associate, Mr. Stone. He always goes the extra mile and look how prosperous he is. Look how many people are going the extra mile for him. There are a lot of people who, if they didn't make good money working for Mr. Stone, they'd pay him a salary just to work for him. I've actually heard one say that he's become immensely wealthy himself working for Mr. Stone. He said, "If I didn't make money out of working for him, I'd pay him if I had to, just for the association with him." Mr. Stone's not different from you or me or anybody else, except in his mental attitude toward people and toward himself. He makes it his business to go the extra mile. Sometimes, people take advantage of that. They don't act fairly with him. I've seen that happen, but he doesn't worry about that too much. In fact, he doesn't worry about anything at all, period. He's learned to adjust himself to life in such a way that he gets great joy out of living and gets great joy out of people. Write a letter to some acquaintance, offering him encouragement. In your job, do a little more than you're paid to do, stay a little longer on the job, or make some other person a little happier.

POINTS TO REMEMBER

1. The reason behind the failure of the majority of people is that they give up easily.
2. Nature requests and demands that every living thing go the extra mile in order to eat, in order to live, and in order to survive.
3. The eternality of the law of increasing returns.

5

ORGANIZED PLANNING

No individual has sufficient experience, education, native ability, and knowledge to ensure the accumulation of a great fortune without the cooperation of other people. Every plan you adopt in your endeavor to accumulate wealth should be the joint creation of yourself and every other member of your Master Mind Group. You may originate your own plans, either in whole or in part, but SEE THAT THOSE PLANS ARE CHECKED, AND APPROVED, BY THE MEMBERS OF YOUR MASTER MIND ALLIANCE.

If the first plan which you adopt does not work successfully, replace it with a new plan. If this new plan fails to work, replace it in turn with still another, and so on until you find a plan which DOES WORK. Right here is the point at which the majority of people meet with failure because of their lack of PERSISTENCE in creating new plans to take the place of those which fail.

The most intelligent individual cannot succeed in

accumulating money—or in any other undertaking—without plans which are practical and workable. Just keep this fact in mind and remember, when your plans fail, that temporary defeat is not permanent failure. It may only mean that your plans have not been sound. Build other plans. Start over again.

Thomas A. Edison "failed" 10,000 times before he perfected the incandescent electric light bulb—that is, he met with *temporary defeat* 10,000 times before his efforts were crowned with success.

Temporary defeat should mean only one thing—the certain knowledge that there is something wrong with your plan. Millions of people go through life in misery and poverty because they lack a sound plan through which to accumulate a fortune.

Henry Ford accumulated a fortune not because of his superior mind, but because he adopted and followed a PLAN which proved to be sound. A thousand individuals could be pointed out, each with a better education than Ford's, yet each of whom lives in poverty because he or she does not possess the RIGHT plan for the accumulation of money.

Your achievement can be no greater than your PLANS are sound. That may seem to be an axiomatic statement, but it is true. And no one is ever whipped until that person QUITS—*in his or her own mind.*

This fact will be repeated many times because it is so easy to "take the count" at the first sign of defeat.

James J. Hill met with temporary defeat when he first endeavored to raise the necessary capital to build a railroad from the East to the West, but he, too, turned defeat into victory *through new plans.*

Henry Ford met with temporary defeat, not only at the beginning of his automobile career, but after he had gone far toward the top. He created new plans and went marching on to financial victory.

We see people who have accumulated great fortunes, but we often recognize only their triumph, overlooking the temporary defeats which they had to surmount before "arriving."

NO FOLLOWER OF THIS PHILOSOPHY CAN REASONABLY EXPECT TO ACCUMULATE A FORTUNE WITHOUT EXPERIENCING TEMPORARY DEFEAT. When defeat comes, accept it as a signal that your plans are not sound, rebuild those plans, and set sail once more toward your coveted goal. If you give up before your goal has been reached, you are a quitter. A QUITTER NEVER WINS— AND A WINNER NEVER QUITS. Lift this sentence out, write it on a piece of paper in letters an inch high, and place it where you will see it every night before you go to sleep and every morning before you go to work.

When you begin to select members for your Master Mind Group, endeavor to select those who do not take defeat seriously.

Some people foolishly believe that only MONEY can make money. This is not true! DESIRE, transmuted into its monetary equivalent, through the principles laid down here, is the agency through which money is made. Money, of itself, is nothing but inert matter. It cannot move, think, or talk, but it can "hear" when a person who DESIRES it calls it to come!

PLANNING THE SALE OF SERVICES

The remainder of this chapter is given over to a description of ways and means of marketing personal services. The information here conveyed will be of practical help to any person having any form of personal services to market, but it will be of priceless benefit to those who aspire to leadership in their chosen occupations.

Intelligent planning is essential for success in any undertaking designed to accumulate riches. The following pages provide detailed instructions to those who must begin the accumulation of riches by selling personal services.

It should be encouraging to know that practically all the great fortunes began in the form of compensation for personal services or from the sale of IDEAS. What else, except ideas and personal services, would one who owns little property have to give in return for riches?

Broadly speaking, there are two types of people in the world. One type is known as LEADERS and the other as FOLLOWERS. Decide at the outset whether you intend to become a leader in your chosen calling or remain a follower. The difference in compensation is vast. The follower cannot reasonably expect the compensation to which a leader is entitled, although many followers make the mistake of expecting such pay.

It is no disgrace to be a follower. On the other hand, it is no credit to remain a follower. Most great leaders began in the capacity of followers. They became great leaders because they were INTELLIGENT FOLLOWERS. With few exceptions, the person who cannot follow a leader intelligently cannot become an efficient leader. The person who can follow a leader most efficiently is usually the one who develops into leadership most rapidly. An intelligent follower has many advantages, among them the OPPORTUNITY TO ACQUIRE KNOWLEDGE FROM HIS OR HER LEADER.

THE 11 MAJOR FACTORS OF LEADERSHIP

The following are important attributes of leadership:

1. UNWAVERING COURAGE based upon knowledge of self and of one's occupation. No follower wishes to be dominated by a leader who lacks self-confidence and courage. No intelligent follower willbe dominated by such a leader very long.
2. SELF-CONTROL. The person who lacks self-control can never control others. Self-control sets a mighty example for one's followers, which the more intelligent will emulate.
3. A KEEN SENSE OF JUSTICE. Without a sense of fairness and justice, no leader can command and retain the respect of his or her followers.
4. DEFINITENESS OF DECISION. Individuals who waver in their decisions show that they are not sure of themselves. They cannot lead others successfully.
5. DEFINITENESS OF PLANS. Successful leaders must plan their work and work their plan. Leaders who move by guesswork, withoutpractical, definite plans, are comparable to a ship without a rudder. Sooner or later they will land on the rocks.
6. THE HABIT OF DOING MORE THAN PAID FOR. One of the penalties of leadership is the necessity of willingness, upon the part of leaders, to do more than they require of their followers.
7. A PLEASING PERSONALITY. No slovenly, careless person can become a successful leader. Leadership calls for respect. Followers will not respect a leader who does not grade high on all of the factors of a "Pleasing Personality."
8. SYMPATHY AND UNDERSTANDING. Successful leaders must be in sympathy with their followers. Moreover, they must understand them and their problems.

9. MASTERY OF DETAIL. Successful leadership calls for mastery of details of the leader's position.
10. WILLINGNESS TO ASSUME FULL RESPONSIBILITY. Successful leaders must be willing to assume responsibility for the mistakes and the shortcomings of their followers. If they try to shift this responsibility, they will not remain the leader. If one of their followers makes a mistake and demonstrates incompetence, leaders must consider that it is *they themselves* who failed.
11. COOPERATION. Successful leaders must understand and apply the principle of cooperative effort and be able to induce their followers to do the same. Leadership calls for POWER and power calls for COOPERATION.

There are two forms of leadership. The first, by far the most effective, is LEADERSHIP BY CONSENT of, and with the sympathy of, the followers. The second is LEADERSHIP BY FORCE, without the consent and sympathy of the followers.

History is filled with evidence that Leadership by Force cannot endure. The downfall and disappearance of dictators and kings is significant. It means that people will not follow forced leadership indefinitely.

The world has just entered a new era of relationship between leaders and followers, which very clearly calls for new leaders and a new brand of leadership in business and industry. Those who belong to the old school of Leadership by Force must acquire an understanding of the new brand of leadership (cooperation) or be relegated to the rank and file of the followers. There is no other way out for them.

The relationship of employer and employee, or of leader and follower, in the future will be one of mutual cooperation, based upon an equitable division of the profits of business. In the future, the relationship of employer and employee will be more like a partnership than it has been in the past. Napoleon, Kaiser Wilhelm of Germany, the Czar of Russia, and the King of Spain were examples of leadership by force. Their leadership passed. Without much difficulty, one might point to the prototypes of these ex-leaders among the business, financial, and labor leaders of America who have been dethroned or slated to go. *Leadership by Consent* (of the followers) is the only brand which can endure!

People may follow the forced leadership temporarily, but they will not do so willingly.

The new brand of LEADERSHIP will embrace the 11 Major Factors of Leadership described in this chapter, as well as some other factors. The individual who makes these the basis of his or her leadership will find abundant opportunity to lead in any walk of life. The difficult economic times we have faced have been prolonged in large part because the world lacked LEADERSHIP of the new brand. Now the demand for leaders who are competent to apply the new methods of leadership has greatly exceeded the supply. Some of the old type of leaders will reform and adapt themselves to the new brand of leadership, but generally speaking, the world will have to look for new timber for its leadership.

This necessity may be your OPPORTUNITY!

THE 10 MAJOR CAUSES OF FAILURE IN LEADERSHIP

We come now to the major faults of leaders who fail, because it is just as essential to know WHAT NOT TO DO as it is to know what to do.

1. INABILITY TO ORGANIZE DETAILS. Efficient leadership calls for ability to organize and to master details. Genuine leaders are never "too busy" to do anything which may be required of them in their capacity as leaders. Whenever people, whether they are leader or follower, admit that they are too busy to change their plans, or to give attention to any emergency, they admit their inefficiency. Successful leaders must be the master of all details connected with their position. That means, of course, that they must acquire the habit of delegating details to capable lieutenants.
2. UNWILLINGNESS TO RENDER HUMBLE SERVICE. Truly great leaders are willing when the occasion demands to perform any sort of labor which they would ask another to perform. "The greatest among ye shall be the servant of all" is a truth which all able leaders observe and respect.
3. EXPECTATION OF PAY FOR WHAT THEY KNOW, INSTEAD OF WHAT THEY *DO* WITH THAT WHICH THEY KNOW. The world does not pay people for that which they know. It pays them forwhat they DO or induce others to do.
4. FEAR OF COMPETITION FROM FOLLOWERS. Leaders who fear that one of their followers may take their position are practically sure to realize that fear sooner or later. Able leaders train understudies to whom they may delegate, at will, any of the details of their position. Only in this way can leaders multiply themselves and prepare themselves to be at many places and give attention to many things at one time. It is an eternal truth that people receive more pay for their
ABILITY TO GET OTHERS TO PERFORM than

they could possibly earn by their own efforts. Efficient leaders may, through their knowledge of their job and the magnetism of their personality, greatly increase the efficiency of others and induce them to render more service and better service than they could render without the leader's aid.

5. LACK OF IMAGINATION. Without imagination, leaders are incapable of meeting emergencies and of creating plans by which to guide their followers efficiently.

6. SELFISHNESS. Leaders who claim all the honor for the work of their followers are sure to be met by resentment. Great leaders CLAIM NONE OF THE HONORS. They are contented to see the honors, when there are any, go to their followers because they know that most people will work harder for commendation and recognition than they will for money alone.

7. INTEMPERANCE. Followers do not respect an intemperate leader. Moreover, intemperance in any of its various forms destroys the endurance and the vitality of all who indulge in it.

8. DISLOYALTY. Perhaps this should have come at the head of the list. Leaders who are not loyal to their trust and to their associates, those above and those below, cannot long maintain their leadership. Disloyalty marks one as being less than the dust of the earth, and brings down on one's head the contempt he or she deserves. Lack of loyalty is one of the major causes of failure in every walk of life.

9. OVEREMPHASIS ON THE AUTHORITY OF LEADERSHIP. Efficient leaders lead by encouraging and not by trying to instill fear in the hearts of their followers.

Leaders who try to impress their followers with their "authority" come within the category of Leadership by Force. If leaders are REAL LEADERS, they will have no need to advertise that fact except by their conduct—their sympathy, understanding, fairness, and a demonstration that they know their job.

10. OVEREMPHASIS ON TITLE. Competent leaders require no title to give them the respect of their followers. The individual who makes too much over his or her title generally has little else to emphasize. The doors to the office of real leaders are open to all who wish to enter, and their working quarters are free from formality or ostentation.

These are among the more common of the causes of failure in leadership. Any one of these faults is sufficient to induce failure. Study the list carefully if you aspire to leadership, and make sure that you are free of these faults.

EIGHT MUSTS FOR AN EFFECTIVE RESUME

A resume should be prepared as carefully as a lawyer would prepare the brief of a case to be tried in court. Unless the applicant is experienced in the preparation of resumes, an expert should be consulted and hired for this purpose. Successful merchants employ men and women who understand the art and the psychology of advertising to present the merits of their merchandise. One who has personal services for sale should do the same. The following eight items of information should appear in the resume:

1. *Education*. State briefly, but specifically, what education you have had and in what subjects you specialized, giving the reasons for thatspecialization.

2. *Experience.* If you have had experience in connection with positions similar to the one you seek, describe it fully, and state names and addresses of former employers. Be sure to bring out clearly any *special* experience you may have had which would equip you to fill the position you seek.
3. *References.* Practically every business firm desires to know all about the previous records, antecedents, etc., of prospective employees who seek positions of responsibility. Attach to your resume photostatic copies of letters from:
   a. former employers
   b. teachers under whom you studied
   c. prominent people whose judgment may be relied upon
4. *Photograph.* Attach to your resume a recent, unmounted photograph of yourself (or, if your resume is being printed professionally, have the photograph suitably reproduced).
5. *Apply for a specific position.* Avoid applying for a position without describing EXACTLY what particular position you seek. Never apply for "just a position." That indicates you lack specialized qualifications.
6. *State your qualifications* for the particular position for which you apply. Give full details as to the reason you believe you are qualified for the particular position you seek. This is THE MOST IMPORTANT DETAIL OF YOUR APPLICATION. It will determine more than anything else what consideration you receive.
7. *Offer to go to work on probation.* In the majority of instances, if you are determined to have the position for which you apply, it will be most effective if you offer to work for a week, or a month, or for a sufficient length of time to enable your prospective employer to judge your

value WITHOUT PAY. This may appear to be a radical suggestion, but experience has proved that it seldom fails to win at least a trial. If you are SURE OF YOUR QUALIFICATIONS, a trial is all you need. Incidentally, such an offer indicates that you have confidence in your ability to fill the position you seek. It is most convincing. If your offer is accepted, and you make good, more than likely you will be paid for your probation period. Make clear the fact that your offer is based upon:
    a. your confidence in your ability to fill the position
    b. your confidence in your prospective employer's decision toemploy you after trial
    c. your DETERMINATION to have the position you seek
8. *Knowledge of your prospective employer's business.* Before applying for a position, do sufficient research in connection with the business to familiarize yourself thoroughly with that business, and indicate in your resume the knowledge you have acquired in this field. This will be impressive, as it will indicate that you have imagination and a real interest in the position you seek.

Remember that it is not the lawyer who knows the most law, but the one who prepares the best case who wins. If your "case" is properly prepared and presented, your victory will have been more than half won at the outset.

Do not be afraid of making your resume too long. Employers are just as much interested in purchasing the services of well-qualified applicants as you are in securing employment. In fact, the success of most successful employers is due mainly to their ability to select well-qualified lieutenants. They want all the information available.

Remember another thing: Neatness and care in the preparation of your resume will indicate that you are a painstaking person. I have helped to prepare resumes for clients which were so striking and out of the ordinary that they resulted in the employment of the applicant without a personal interview.

Successful salespeople groom themselves with care. They understand that first impressions are lasting. Your resume is your sales representative. Give it a good suit of clothes so it will stand out in bold contrast to anything your prospective employer ever saw in the way of an application for a position. If the position you seek is worth having, it is worth going after with care. Moreover, if you sell yourself to employers in a manner that impresses them with your individuality, you may very well receive more money for your services from the very start than you would if you applied for employment in the usual way.

If you seek employment through an employment agency, make sure they use copies of your resume—or produce and provide one that meets all the above criteria—in marketing your services. This will help to gain preference for you both with the agency and prospective employers.

HOW TO GET THE EXACT POSITION YOU DESIRE

Everyone enjoys doing the kind of work for which they are best suited. An artist loves to work with paints, a craftsman with his or her hands, a writer loves to write. Those with less definite talents have their preferences for certain fields of business or industry. If America does anything well, it offers a full range of occupations, from tilling the soil and manufacturing, to marketing, commerce, and the professions.

Here are seven actions to take to guarantee yourself the exact position you wish:

First. Decide—and DEFINE briefly in writing—EXACTLY what kind of job you desire. If the job does not already exist, perhaps you can create it.

Second. Choose the specific company, or the specific individual, for whom you wish to work.

Third. Study your prospective employer as to policies, personnel, and chances of advancement.

Fourth. By analysis of yourself, your talents and capabilities, figure WHAT YOU CAN OFFER and plan ways and means of giving advantages, services, developments, and ideas that *you believe* you can successfully deliver.

Fifth. Forget about "a job." Forget whether or not there is an opening. Forget the usual routine of "have you got a job for me?" Concentrate on what *you can give*.

Sixth. Once you have your plan in mind, arrange with an experienced writer to put it on paper, in neat form and in full detail.

Seventh. Present it to the *proper person with authority* and he or she will do the rest. Every company is looking for people who can givesomething of value, whether it be ideas, services, or "connections." Every company has room for the individual who has a definite plan of action which is to the advantage of that company.

This line of procedure may take a few days or weeks of extra time, but the difference in income, in advancement, and in gaining recognition will save years of hard work at small pay. It has many advantages, the main one being that it will often save from one to five years of time in reaching a chosen goal.

Every person who starts, or "gets in," halfway up the ladder does so by deliberate and careful planning (excepting, of course, the Boss' kid.)

POINTS TO REMEMBER

1. Even the most intelligent man can't succeed in becoming wealthy unless he has a practical plan.
2. If you face failure then that is your sign to alter your plan.
3. There are only two types of people in the world—leaders and followers.

6

SELF CONTROL

Self-control is the balance wheel that directs your *action* so that it will build up and not tear down.

To be a person who is well "balanced," you must be a person in whom *enthusiasm* and *self-control* are equalized. A survey which I have just completed of the 160,000 adult inmates of the penitentiaries of the United States discloses the startling fact that ninety-two per cent of these unfortunate men and women are in prison because they lacked the necessary *self-control* to direct their energies constructively.

Read the foregoing paragraph again; it is authentic, it is *startling!*

It is a fact that the majority of a man's griefs come about through lack of *self-control.* The holy scriptures are full of admonition in support of *self-control.* They even urge us to love our enemies and to forgive those who injure us. The law of non-resistance runs, like a golden cord, throughout the Bible.

Study the records of those whom the world calls great, and observe that *every one of them possesses this quality of self-control!*

For example, study the characteristics of our own immortal Lincoln. In the midst of his most trying hours he exercised patience, poise and *self-control.* These were some of the qualities which made him the great man that he was. He found disloyalty in some of the members of his cabinet; but, for the reason that this disloyalty was toward him, personally, and because those in whom he found it had qualities which made them valuable to his country, Lincoln exercised *self-control* and disregarded the objectionable qualities.

How many men do you know who have *self-control* to equal this?

In language more forceful than it was polished, Billy Sunday exclaimed from the pulpit: *"There is something as rotten as hell about the man who is always trying to show some other fellow up!"* I wonder if the "devil" didn't yell, "Amen, brother!" when Billy made that statement?

However, *self-control* becomes an important factor in this Reading Course on the Law of Success, not so much because lack of it works hardships on those who become its victims, as for the reason that those who do not exercise it suffer the loss of a great power which they need in their struggle for achievement of their *definite chief aim.*

If you neglect to exercise *self-control,* you are not only likely to injure others, but you are *sure to injure yourself!*

POINTS TO REMEMBER

1. A well-balanced person is someone in whom self-control and enthusiasm are present in equal proportion.
2. Direct your actions with self-control.
3. Learn to love your enemies and forgive those who hurt you.

7

WILL YOU MASTER MONEY? OR WILL IT MASTER YOU?

Anything that robs you of peace of mind robs you of life's greatest wealth. You may lose peace of mind by pursuing money too anxiously, or by trying to acquire more money than you can spend wisely. Money you earn through constructive work is the money most likely to benefit you. It is a mistake to deprive young people of the need to know life through work. Anyone can save, and the effort you make toward saving a percentage of your income gives you a true knowledge of the value of money. Saving also prepares you to handle many opportunities which otherwise might slip by.

In my explorations of the points of view of young people I rarely find a great appreciation of money, most especially when a good sum of money is yet to be earned. This is proper enough. A lack of money makes the business of living so difficult it is very likely to destroy peace of mind.

So the young man pursues money. For a good part of his life he is likely to have no difficulty whatsoever in spending as much as he makes. If he has a family, they help him spend it. A successful man, however, is not very old before he begins to accumulate some money beyond his immediate needs and his household bank account. This money is likely to go into investments, real estate and the like.

Be he a truly positive-minded man, he will soon own considerable amounts of both property and money. And somewhere along the line he will have passed an invisible border. He is now rich in the sense that he has a considerable surplus above his needs. Undoubtedly he can fulfill any reasonable want. And so, while his financial records show he is rich, his inward and very private record should show he has peace of mind.

He will have peace of mind—if he has mastered money. He will not—if money has mastered him.

A man who makes a big splash may be a man who has gone overboard. The "big splash" is the big show of one's material wealth. I have freely admitted my own weakness for making a big splash in the days of my Catskill estate which I was fortunate enough to lose before it permanently harmed me. Not every man is endangered by making a vast show of his wealth, and some seem to thrive on it. Others enter upon such conspicuous display that obviously they have gone overboard—their souls are drowning in their sea of dollars.

Some years ago a man who had earned several million dollars suddenly went bankrupt. When the lawyers searched his assets, they found a large warehouse filled with valuable antique furniture, magnificent paintings and the like. They all belonged to the man who was bankrupt and he had paid for them in cash. But had he ever enjoyed them? Most of those precious items never had been unpacked! He liked to talk about his treasures, however, and make himself sound like a veritable Croesus. Such an accumulation mania is at the opposite pole from a mind that knows peace.

"They are going to take it away from me!" The fear of poverty has a strange and ugly first cousin. It is the rich man's fear that his money will be taken away from him; or that he will not be allowed to pile up his money into ten times the sum he possibly could use—twenty times—thirty times!

I once knew a majority stockholder of the fabulous CocaCola Company. He had gathered money in many ways, and was worth about twenty-five million dollars. Did he have peace of mind? He had a mind filled with hatred and mistrust. His worst hatred was directed toward the government. Although he was then well in his eighties, he always prophesied that the government would cause him to die a pauper.

The last time I ever saw him, he asked me a most significant question: "If you were in my place, what would you do to protect your peace of mind and save your money?"

I had determined that for the sake of my own peace of mind I never would start a quarrel with this man; but, if he ever asked me a direct question, he would receive a direct answer. Even so, I asked him now if he wanted my honest opinion. "Yes!" he said. "Naturally!"

"Well," said I, "if I were in your place and wanted peace of mind I would not save my money. Your peace of mind and your money have become enemies who cannot live side by side. If I were you, I would first convert all my money into United States Savings Bonds so that it would go to work for the benefit of all the people. Then I would pile all those bonds into my fireplace and set fire to them. And as I watched my money go up the chimney, I would watch a great deal of my unhappiness burn away."

My friend snapped, "Don't be facetious!'

"I was never more serious in my life," I replied. "If I had your fortune and it deprived me of my peace of mind, I would first put my money where it would be well distributed and then I would burn every symbol of my government's debt to me. Then I would go to bed and sleep like a child and wake up feeling peaceful and free."

I did not expect this man to follow my advice. To the day he died he lived in fear and bitterness, and I believe that the illness and debility which dogged him long before he died was rooted in his love—not of mankind, but of money.

PEACE OVER POWER

There are very few people for whom advice to burn their money would be good advice. The principle is what holds for every one of us. Nothing, absolutely nothing is as precious as your peace of mind. Few young people see this. Some people see it as they gain more experience. Many never see it. Remember, you can be rich with peace of mind, but if money or anything else gets in the way of your peace of mind, choose peace of mind and let the other go.

Notice I made no attempt to evaluate my friend's complaint against the government. His complaint may in some ways have been justified. It was his attitude I drove at—an attitude of fear and distrust while he was at least twenty-five times a millionaire and could have done so much toward making himself and others happy.

How much money does a man need? Andrew Carnegie certainly had a firm hold on methods for making money. In his later years, his earnest wish was to give this "know-how" to the average man. Mr. Carnegie was one of the first of the enlightened industrialists who saw how important it is for a nation to spread its wealth.

He saw that millions can be rich in the sense of having plenty. He also saw that, in the nature of things, the man who has millions always will be an exception. He saw that a goal of "millions" of even "a million" is not the right goal for the majority of men. For many, such a goal sets up strains which deny peace of mind. They may give up too much that is necessary for men of their personality, and so end with nothing. He admonished me again and again to make this clear, and I have done my best to do so.

How much money, then, does a man need?

As much as will keep him and his loved ones in what he considers solid comfort, along with enough luxury so that he may feel he has tasted the treats of life.

Aiming for this, and always maintaining his peace of mind, he conditions himself to a full use of his self-confident faith. And out of this conditioning he often finds a moneymaking power beyond his dreams. For such a man, excess money never will be a curse. He knows how to live, so he knows how to broaden his life. He has never tried to cheat others, so he knows how to help others.

The man who wanted a hundred billion dollars. A student of mine once flew all the way from India to have an interview with me. First he sent me a letter in which he stated that his major purpose in life was to accumulate one hundred times as much wealth as Henry Ford had accumulated, or about one hundred billion dollars. He wished to be one hundred thousand times a millionaire.

When at length we sat in my study, I asked him what he would do with that modest little sum of money.

After some hesitation, he admitted: "Honestly, I don't know." "Well," I said, "the possession of one hundred billion dollars by one individual poses a threat to the world. But let us put that aside. If you desired to spend the sum in helping the people of India overcome the superstitions and outmoded customs which have held them in bondage for centuries, I'd have some sympathy with you. It seems to me that you just want the money for the sake of outdoing Henry Ford."

He thought awhile and admitted this was so. I helped him search himself, and he saw that in using the Science of Personal Achievement he had "taken the bit in his teeth" and was galloping beyond control. What the mind builds in imagination, the mind can indeed build in reality; but we speak of a mind in good balance. Discussing his affairs, he came to see that a quarter of a million dollars would buy him what he really wanted. With that realization, the tense businessman—he was an importer—relaxed and said he felt much better.

This story's sequel involves another of those "coincidences" I do not believe are really coincidences. Before this man returned to India I helped him secure several contracts for the sale of American-made products in his homeland. His profit eventually amounted to just a little over a quarter of a million dollars.

Money that benefits you most often comes from work that benefits you. In the last chapter I planted the idea that one can ensure that his money and property go to persons of his choice when he dies. Unlike death itself, the bequeathing of assets is a controllable circumstance.

You are going to make money; and when you do, please be careful that such a bequest does not rob an inheritor of his peace of mind.

It has been said, and with reason, that a rich man's son often does not display the ability his father had. I believe that many rich men's sons are robbed of this ability because they inherit their fathers' money. By and large, the "old man" worked for his money. His money came to him side by side with the development of his insight, his ability, his knowledge of people and his knowledge of the world. He was not given riches by his father; he was given riches by his work.

Now let us look at the son. All his life he has lived in the midst of money and the many comforts which money buys. He knows he is going to inherit great amounts of money. Assuming that he does have the inherent willingness to work hard—what happens to that willingness? In many cases it is replaced by a willingness to get something for nothing, and thus he never learns one of the basic lessons of life.

Great fortunes or modest fortunes are a blessing only when they are used in good part to benefit others. No father benefits his son when he robs him of initiative. No testator favors a beneficiary by making it unnecessary for him to work. You may wish to shield your inheritors from the meanness of poverty. Well and good! Beyond that, do not shield them from life with a wall of money. Let them have the priceless opportunity of building better lives with their own life-taught wisdom and their own constructive work.

In my youth I worked as a secretary to a wealthy lawyer who had two sons somewhat older than myself. These youths attended the University of Virginia. It became my duty to make up for each of them a monthly check for one hundred dollars as spending money. In those days a hundred dollars would buy three or four times what it will today. How I envied those boys!

When I had been in business college, learning how to earn

my own living, I had often gone hungry because I literally did not have a cent in my pocket. I vividly recall standing in front of a store and longing for some apples which were priced six for a dime. At length I went in and sold the storekeeper on the idea of trusting me for the dime until I got through school and began to earn money. Such were my memories as I made out those magnificent monthly checks.

By and by my employer's sons came home with their diplomas. They also came home conditioned to easy living and with little idea of what work is all about. Were they inherently as capable as their father? We shall never know. One of them was put into a good job in a bank his father owned, and another was made manager of one of his father's coal mines.

Ten years later they had completely wrecked their father's fortune and his health as well.

I no longer envy anyone, for envy is no part of peace of mind. As I look back, I am grateful that I had to undergo such experiences as negotiating a ten-cent long-term credit. And I am grateful that, when I began to earn money, my earning power became part of my self-fulfillment. I am even glad that when I made mistakes and lost money, I had no rich father to see me through, for I found a mighty teacher in adversity.

My book *Think and Grow Rich* has been read by perhaps seven million men and women. In the twenty years since it was published I have been able to talk to some of these people, and I see that some have used the book to help them become truly rich. But some have used it to help them become rich in money only.

THE TWELVE GREAT RICHES OF LIFE

1. A positive mental attitude
2. Sound physical health
3. Harmony in human relationships
4. Freedom from all forms of fear
5. The hope of future achievement
6. The capacity for faith
7. A willingness to share one's blessings
8. A labor of love as an occupation
9. An open mind on all subjects
10. Self-discipline in all circumstances
11. The capacity to understand others
12. Sufficient money

These are the riches which can and should go along with peace of mind. Notice I have set money in the last place, and this despite my insisting that it is very difficult to have peace of mind without sufficient money. I set it there because you yourself will automatically give emphasis to money. Now and then, therefore, I must remind you to de-emphasize it and remember this: Money will buy a great deal but it will not buy peace of mind—it only will help you find peace of mind. But neither money nor anything else can help you find peace of mind unless you begin the journey from within yourself.

BASIC STEPS IN BUILDING YOUR INCOME

I have been told that it is not good logic to warn people of the dangers of misusing money, when probably they do not have enough money to make them worry about misusing it. I would follow this advice if I were writing a book merely about how to earn money. This book also is concerned with showing you where you are going and how the world looks when you get there. It helps you build correct attitudes right at the start.

As long as we have pointed firmly at those attitudes, however—as we shall point again—I shall set down some practical ways in which a person who has little or no capital can begin to build his wealth. Each of these ways is specific unto itself, so to speak, but is capable of almost infinite modification. It is up to you to pause as you read and apply these procedures to yourself, your talents, your surroundings and, above all, your goals.

1. Get other people to help their own businesses by helping yours. A young life insurance salesman was having trouble in placing policies with heads of families. Using this adversity as a springboard, he wondered why he could not sell insurance to the very same men, not in their role as heads of families but in their role as businessmen. After all, money taken out of the family budget is money gone; but a business expense offers an opportunity of bringing back the expended sum many times over.

He began with a leading restaurant owner in his town. He pointed out to this man that he might very well advertise that the food he served was so wholesome and sustaining that people who ate in his restaurant were likely to live longer. The restaurateur said this was indeed so and he intended to make sure it always was so. Good, said the insurance man, and explained the rest of the plan. The restaurateur was to offer to insure the life of each regular customer for one thousand dollars. Details were worked out and the offer made the restaurant's business boom. Needless to say, it helped the young insurance man.

He extended the idea to a group of filling stations, to a large grocery and to others. I am not positive it was this man who originated the idea of adding life insurance to mortgages so that the mortgage would be paid off if the purchaser died—but he certainly made good use of this angle as well.

Now stop and think: How can you get other people to help their own businesses by helping yours?

2. Show someone how he can get more for his money. Here we are not talking about setting yourself up as a business adviser, so that people seek you out to learn how they can get more for their money. We assume that the initiative must be yours.

Here is how one man did it:

Working at a low salary for a distributor of magazines, he took notice of many different kinds of printing. As with another man I have mentioned in this book, he noticed that many of the printing jobs could have been done with more taste and style.

Now, this young chap was discovering that most jobs of any kind are not done as well as they could be. Take note of this, for a fortune can be made on the idea.

The young man found out more about printing, then went to a large printing firm. He arranged to bring in printing jobs at a 10 per cent commission. He then went to large users of printed matter and collected a great many samples, which he took home and studied.

Selecting two or three brochures which obviously needed improvement, he arranged with a freelance commercial artist to prepare a sample layout for each, on the promise of a fair fee if the job went through. An advertising copywriter who had spare time contributed his own talents on the same basis. Armed now with a good "rough" of an improved job, the young man took the brochures to the firms which had issued them and simply showed how much better they could be.

Now, let us look into some of the practical psychology at work here.

To begin with, a person or a company may go on almost forever with some condition or process or product that "gets by." He may not realize he is merely getting by; or if he does, he is too busy or too lazy to do anything about it.

Along comes someone who makes him dissatisfied with what he has and in the same moment shows him how to do better. Moreover, the work is all done for him. Why not take advantage of it?

Now stop and think: How can you show someone how he can get more for his money? Extend that: How can you help someone get more for his money in such a way that he will thereafter depend on you to show him again and again?

3. Bring producer and consumer together. The farmer used to have a tough time bringing his goods to market. Imagine an isolated farm in hilly country, on a road that was mostly mud, and with horse and wagon the only means of transportation, Still, the farmer had to bring his produce to town and so he did by hook or by crook.

Everything in our economy intermeshes with everything else. As the automobile came in, roads had to be improved and they were. Now the farmer could carry his goods five to ten times the distance he used to and still get home the same night. Soon someone found he could set up marketing centers between towns, and draw on the increasing car traffic for customers while the farmers were very glad to be a continued source of supply.

Farmers used to depend on peddlers who came by perhaps

twice a year, sometimes on foot with huge packs on their backs. Unrolling his pack on the kitchen table, the peddler would provide the farmer's wife with needles and the like, the farmer with tobacco and fish hooks—and above all, with news. How hungry people used to be for news! The peddlers invariably had more money than the farmers, for they performed the valuable function of bringing producer and consumer together.

When the farmer wanted to sell or buy a horse, he often was assisted by a broker who helped both parties reach an agreement on price, then sealed the bargain by making them shake hands. The broker, too, generally made more money than the farmers because he brought producer and consumer together.

Recently I read of complaints by shoppers in the Soviet Union. It seems they spend endless hours standing on line in front of separate, specialized food stores. Eventually they may adopt the American idea of bringing many producers and many consumers together in convenient supermarkets.

Fortunes have been made in this revolution in merchandising, especially as supermarkets—and their sprawling parking lots—have moved into the suburbs and even far out into the country. Fringe benefits have come to many property owners who saw how to ride along with the trend.

A woman lived alone on twenty poor acres which had mostly been taken over by scrub pine. At last she decided to sell the old homestead. Neighbors told her, sighing, that she would never get much for it. A local real estate man made her a pitiable offer.

This woman, however, was one of those elderly (in years) people who never had seen any reason why her mind should not remain alert. She told herself that her farm must be good for something. She decided to spend thirty days in an intensive investigation of what run-down farms are good for. Before the end of that thirty days she had found she could sell it as a base for a riding stable, complete with pasture and pleasant riding trails, for twice what the real estate man had offered.

But also she had studied several supermarkets in the area and had concluded that her farm would make a good supermarket site. She sold out finally to a supermarket for five times what the real estate man had offered.

When roads were paved and transportation by automobile became so easy, it was predicted that the mail-order house would disappear. After all, why should a person buy from a catalog when he can buy from the store itself? Such firms as Sears, Roebuck and Montgomery Ward nevertheless continue to flourish.

Despite constant rises in postage rates, thousands of mailorder businesses thrive on selling everything from postage scales with the new rates printed on them, to books, household furnishings, preserved and fresh food, vitamins, equipment for hobbies, boat supplies...the list is almost endless.

Why is this so? Because times may change but universal needs always continue. Showing a person that he can write his name and address on an order form and drop it into the mail, and be assured of prompt delivery of something he wants, continues to be a good way to bring producer and consumer together.

Sometimes the producer sells directly to the consumer. Far more often the consumer buys from a middle man who assumes retail selling as his special function or from a manufacturer's representative.

Now stop and think: How can you bring producer and consumer together?

Some of the money you earn should stay with you. Certainly we have not exhausted the subject of making money! You may even feel that in giving the subject a once-overlightly treatment, I have not done justice to it. I suggest, however, that you reread the foregoing three items and see in how many ways you can relate yourself to them. They have a great universality. Stretch them—you need not be too literal—and you will find they cover a vast variety of business situations, a broad horizon of opportunities. Note that they have not been tied to any particular craft or skill, since the fields mentioned are illustrative of many others.

You will find it an interesting exercise to see how many incidents of your own affairs can be fitted into one or more of those three categories. If you will put aside your own work and see yourself as a consumer, you certainly will "fit"! We shall touch upon many other principles which help hard-working men make money.

We still are talking about money and peace of mind.

Nobody who goes too deeply into debt can count on having peace of mind. You may have it for a time, but now and again the debt comes into your consciousness and you feel you are not quite your own master; somebody else owns a piece of you. I am not talking here of ordinary business credit without which business hardly could exist, but more of personal debts.

Having some money laid away is a means of avoiding the uncertainty and often the embarrassment that goes with incurring a personal debt. But saving does more for you than merely make it possible to spend the money you save. Saving gives you the habit of gauging your money against your needs. It helps to remind you that money is good only because of what it can buy in goods and services, and again it helps you gauge what you need in the way of goods and services.

> **POINTS TO REMEMBER**
>
> 1. Peace of mind is life's greatest wealth.
> 2. Money that benefits you most often comes from work that benefits you.
> 3. Never ending greed for money will lead to your downfall.

8

HOW TO DEVELOP YOUR OWN HEALTHY EGO

All your ability and personality show themselves in your ego. For many a man the ego works always at full power and for some it needs restraining. For most, it is as well to find and use some ego-boosting device. Your own ego-booster may be connected with the way you dress, the way you express yourself, your surroundings, some object which has symbolic value—or in some other way which has a special, individual meaning.

The ego can be attuned to mysterious forces beyond one's self. Through your ego you can be guided toward an expression of yourself which reflects in your increased prosperity.

I have spoken before and shall speak again on the need for knowing your own mind and going in your own direction. Now let us look at the ego, that invaluable mind spark-plug which my dictionary defines as "the self-assertive tendency of man."

People who have peace of mind also have healthy egos.

Now, to some the term "healthy ego" brings to mind the picture of a loud, back-slapping type of person. This may be so, but it is not necessarily so. Your ego as you reflect it to the world has been built for many years out of childhood influences, later influences and a great many other factors. Your ego is as individual as your fingerprints, and what is "healthy" to you will not be healthy for another man.

Often ego seems to have a bit of vanity in it; but it is far stronger and far more subtle than ordinary human vanity. Think of your ego as an invisible part of yourself which makes you strong and resourceful, or puts obstacles in your way, according to the sort of influence you feed it.

Even the greatest of minds now and then find themselves with a rundown ego. Truly great men feel this, and quickly restore their egos. The purpose of this chapter is to show you some of the surprisingly straightforward ego-boosters which others have used, and to give you an assortment out of which you may choose and perfect a tailor-made ego-booster of your own.

The ego that was stronger than a clean shirt and a shave. It is old advice and good advice to say that being well-dressed and well-groomed gives a boost to your ego.

Now I want you to meet a man who knew that very well—but whose deeply abiding ego was strong enough to rise above a clean shirt and a shave.

The impact of this story will be stronger if I tell it in sequence as it came to me. It begins with my meeting Edwin C. Barnes when he was Thomas Edison's business associate. Mr. Barnes at that time owned thirty-one expensively tailored suits and in the course of a month never wore one suit two days in a row. His shirts were made to order out of the most expensive fabrics available. His ties were made to order in Paris and cost at least twenty-five dollars apiece.

One day I suggested jokingly to Mr. Barnes that he let me know when he was ready to discard some of his suits so that I might wear them.

"I know you are kidding," Barnes said, "but you might like to know that at the time I decided to associate myself with Thomas Edison, I didn't have the railroad fare to take me to East Orange, New Jersey, where I had to go to sell him the idea.

"My desire to get there was greater than my fear of the humiliation I would suffer by riding a freight train. I packed a suitcase—it didn't take long—and I traveled by boxcar.

"When I walked into Mr. Edison's office and said I wanted to see him, I heard a titter of laughter all over the place. Finally his secretary consented to let me see Mr. Edison. As soon as I faced the great inventor I started telling him how fortunate he was that I was giving him the first chance at my services. After I'd talked a while, he rose, walked all around me, looked me over with penetrating eyes, grinned and asked: 'What did you come to see me about, young man?'

"That's how I discovered he was hard of hearing. Now I had to explain myself all over, loudly. My clothes were wrinkled and dusty, my shoes were scuffed, I had a two days' growth of beard, and I almost lost my courage. It is to Mr. Edison's credit that he did not judge me by my appearance. But I made up my mind, then and there, that never again would I stand before any man without knowing that I was better dressed than he.

"Now you see why I have all these clothes. And as far as my giving you my discards is concerned, I doubt if you would get from them the same ego boost they give me."

He was right. I never have felt the need to bolster my ego by personal adornment, and I too am right, for ego is a strictly personal matter. During the early part of my career I did stimulate my ego with that large estate and those elegant cars. Later, when my work became widely accepted, I became content with a much simpler style of living. Yet I do not neglect my ego, which functions through my Princes of Guidance.

Still, just like Mr. Barnes and so many others, I see myself reflecting long-ago experiences which I no longer wish to suffer. During my childhood I lived amid poverty and illiteracy, surrounded by poverty-stricken neighbors. Now I am very sensitive to the "feel" of any neighborhood in which I live and it must be just right. I even inspect the approaches to my home to make sure they do not lead through any unpleasant areas.

EARLY FOOTSTEPS ETCH A PERMANENT MARK

You may find it instructive to look back at the early influences of your own life and see how much they may have to do with your actions now. Here are some questions to get you started. Think a while after each to make sure you have found the right answer. As a child...

Did you have sufficient food, clothing and shelter?

If the answer is No; was it insufficient by any reasonable standard or insufficient by some neighborhood or other standard by which you have come to judge?

Did your parents, or someone else who had influence in your life, tend to belittle you and make you feel that your brothers and sisters or playmates were better or smarter than you?

Were you called basically bad when you misbehaved or were your actions merely labeled as unacceptable?

If you were bad by definition, did you decide you were going to live up to your badness?

Did you have sufficient schooling in the three R's so that

you never had to feel inferior, later, about your Reading, Writing and 'rithmetic?

Are you too short, too tall or too fat, so that you feel conspicuous?

Are you exceptionally ill-favored as to appearance, or scarred or crippled?

How would you describe the general atmosphere in your childhood home? Peaceful? Antagonistic? Clouded by worry? Cheerful? Carelessly happy-go-lucky?

Did your parents quarrel in your presence?

Were you conscious of people using you as an "easy mark" or a "push-around"?

Were you fond of being the leader in games and clubs?

Did you set up a symbol of success early in life, such as "a big house like Mr. Jones's" or "a job traveling to glamorous places like Mr. Brown's"?

Did your parents encourage you to accept responsibility—or were they overanxious to do everything for you?

Were you forced to be so much on your own that you never felt you had anyone who really cared what happened to you?

Thinking about such questions will suggest many facets of your past which show themselves in your present actions. I do not suggest you worry about your past; remember, when we close the door on the past we close out a great deal which otherwise might hamper us. At times, however, an understanding of past influences helps you to appreciate and enjoy your present ways of bucking up your ego.

A salesman sells through his ego. While I was engaged in organizing the Science of Personal Achievement, I made my living by training salesmen. More than 30,000 men and women came under my guidance while they were being trained to sell.

The first thing I taught my students was that before any salesman sells anything to anyone, he first must sell it to himself. That is, he must so condition his own ego that it is in shape to strengthen his statements, and he must believe that both he and his product are *good*.

An executive of the New York Life Insurance Company gave me an interesting case. One man had been with the company more than thirty years, and had maintained a high selling record. Suddenly his production dropped to almost nothing. The salesman could not tell what was wrong and neither could the company executives. They called me in to doctor the "patient."

I went out with this salesman to observe him in action. Soon I noticed that his basic trouble, after thirty years in the field, was the fear that he had grown too old for selling. He talked constantly about his age. His fear had developed into hypochondria and he felt he must use a walking stick to help him get around.

Somehow he had persuaded himself that he "didn't have it" any longer and so he expected to be rebuffed. He had allowed his ego to become so thoroughly subdued that he anticipated a *No* before he ever heard it-and that is the best way to make sure it is said!

Back in the office I said to this man: "I want you to go out and find one of those old-fashioned ear trumpets which once were used by the hard-of-hearing."

He protested, "But I am not hard of hearing."

"That's right," I said. "You hear too well. You hear the *No* before it is said. Now, I want you to simulate deafness. Place the trumpet at your ear when anyone speaks, pretend you didn't hear him and when he says *No* go right ahead with your sales talk."

We agreed that he could not sell life insurance to someone

who really did not need it or want it, so nobody would be hurt. He found a monstrous old hearing trumpet and took it with him on his rounds. In his first week as a trumpet-user he procured applications from six out of nine prospective buyers. The next week he came back with eight applications out of twelve interviews—an almost unheard-of record. His ego restored to the *Yes* habit, he put away the trumpet and had no trouble thereafter.

Although my own hearing is fine, I seem often to come into contact with hearing troubles. My son, Blair, was born without ears. How I helped Nature give him sufficient hearing is another story; I am thinking now of the time when we sent him to public school wearing his hair long enough to hide the absence of ears. The other children made fun of his long hair, which was damaging to his ego. We promptly had his hair cut short; but first I sold Blair the idea that his affliction would be a great benefit to him when people understood about it. And that is exactly what happened, for people now were kind to him. He soon lost all self-consciousness about being different from people who have ears.

Perhaps I was inspired by Thomas A. Edison's determination to make an asset out of his deafness rather than a liability. I never saw him wear an expression of annoyance or disappointment. Rather, his expression clearly said: "My ego is under my control and it does my bidding without fear or limitation."

Your ego and your opulence. As with the ear trumpet, I have on many occasions been able to prescribe exactly the right ego-builder for a particular person. It requires knowing the person, of course; and when you wish to prescribe for yourself, you will see the importance of that ancient, great advice: *Know thyself.*

Now and again a man will stop working before he should,

and find himself at loose ends. This was the case with a former student of mine named Ray Cunliffe. He had owned a Cadillac agency in Chicago, which he sold at a handsome profit. Since he now had plenty of liquid assets he decided to take a year and play around and "rest up," as he put it.

Before the year was out he grew restless. He looked around for a good Cadillac franchise, but found none. Another six months passed and he began to eat deeply into his cash reserve for living expenses. About that time he joined a class in the Science of Personal Achievement which I was teaching in Baltimore.

Ray and his wife had been accustomed to having servants in their home. Now they had had to let the servants go and do their own housework. One day while Ray was in the basement doing the family laundry, it occurred to him that he was making the very mistake I had mentioned at a recent lesson. He wasn't nourishing his ego. He was starving it; beating it down.

In his excitement and anxiety he came to me for personal help. He told me his story, then asked, "Where do I go from here?"

He had told me that for several years his wife had wanted a mink coat which would cost some three thousand dollars. Also I could see that although he drove a Cadillac it was beginning to look shabby; and so did the clothes he wore.

So I said: "Ray, get out your notebook and pencil while I give you a prescription for opulence.

"Number One: Go to the nearest Cadillac agency, trade in your present car and buy a new car of the model you like best.

"Number Two: Go to the best fur store in town and buy your wife a fine mink coat, even if it costs more than three thousand dollars.

"Number Three: Go to your tailor and have a complete

wardrobe of suits made up. Then buy the ties and shirts and shoes you need to go with your new suits.

"Number Four: Have the mink coat done up in gift wrapping. Place the package in your new Cadillac, hire a liveried chauffeur, and while you are not at home have the chauffeur drive the car to your house and deliver it and the package to your wife.

"Take these four steps immediately. Then come back for the next prescription; that is, if you need another. This one prescription may turn the tide very quickly."

When the new Cadillac and the mink coat arrived at Ray's home, his wife at first refused to accept them. The chauffeur merely handed her the car keys and walked away, leaving the car in the driveway with the coat on its seat.

Ray's wife finally tried on the coat. Sure enough, it was the very coat she had tried on out of curiosity—and longing—a few weeks earlier.

Suddenly she felt a surge of confidence and happiness. The same thing was happening to Ray. Now, what I have to tell you seemed like magic to him and it may seem like magic to you, but it was not magic.

The cook and the housemaid who formerly worked for the Cunliffes showed up and asked if they might return to their old jobs. Without the slightest hesitation, Mrs. Cunliffe told them to come right in.

As for Ray himself: A friend phone him and said: "I hear that the Baltimore Cadillac Agency can be bought. You might look it over."

Ray looked it over and saw it was good. The deal required $150,000, however, which was quite a sum for him to raise on short notice. His ego had lifted itself out of the doldrums. He said: "I don't know who is going to let me have the money, but I know that I shall get it."

The following day he called on a man he had been avoiding—a wealthy man toward whom he had begun to feel inferior. No inferiority marred his approach now as he explained he needed $150,000 to put himself back into business.

"Fine!" was the answer. "I'm glad to see you getting back into the business where you always made money." He wrote Ray a check for $150,000 and added, "You can pay this back year by year as your profits come in."

So Ray Cunliffe was back in a Cadillac agency of his own and doing a good business almost before he had had time to wear all his new shirts. He had only one disappointment; he was disappointed that I did not show surprise over his sudden turn of fortune.

"Well, Ray," I said, "I can't get excited over something I have seen happen hundreds of times." But I was pleased, of course, to see once more that poverty-consciousness can be replaced by success-consciousness which invariably draws success as though with an all-powerful magnet. Ego is the key to this—an ego filled with self-confident faith, and bolstered by the means that it is right for you.

You can paint an ego-picture of yourself and use it for first-aid. Sometimes a man faces a single situation on which a great deal depends. Often such a situation involves another person who must in some way be persuaded—for whom some situation must be made attractive. When you know that other person, often you can use the power of your ego to give him the picture he wants to see. Even when you do not know him personally, you often can look closely at the values of the situation and come up with a picture that is attractive to him.

Let us now look at myself at a stage in my career when

my ego faltered.

I have told how I was associated with Don Mellett, the newspaper publisher, and how his murder forced the postponement of publication of my first manuscripts; also how it saved me from wearing a Big Business label.

As I related, I had to get out of town to hide from the thugs who believed I had been involved in the attacks upon their illegal rum-running. In the time I spent hiding, my spirits were not good. I came close to losing my faith in my ability to carry out the great task Andrew Carnegie had assigned me some twenty years before.

I took hold of myself and decided to break the bondage of fear. I would find a new publisher. Since Judge Gary had died, I had to start from scratch—not an easy task for the unknown author of a trail-blazing work.

As my ego rebuilt itself and my success-consciousness reasserted itself, an insistent inner voice began to tell me that I would find my publisher in Philadelphia. I knew no publisher in that city, but the inner voice became so strong that on a capital of fifty dollars I got into my car and headed toward the Quaker City, half believing I would find the solution to my problem, half believing I was going mad.

Once in Philadelphia I began to look through a classified telephone directory. I hoped to find a cheap boardinghouse where I could stay for a couple of dollars a day. Now, follow closely what happened, for this story is one of the most startling you ever may read, and it contains—besides its revelation of the power of ego—a revelation of the Supreme Secret that can transform your life.

As I turned the pages of the directory, that inner voice spoke again. It said: "Never mind looking for a cheap boardinghouse. Go to the best hotel in the city and register for the best suite of rooms in the house."

I closed the book and blinked my eyes. I had less than thirty-five dollars in my pocket! But the command was so irresistible that I picked up my luggage, marched to the best hotel in town and took a suite which cost twenty-five dollars a day.

The moment I signed the register, I knew I had done the right thing. My ego and my faith swelled within me. I could not then have put the Supreme Secret into words, but I know it took hold of me.

A quarter was a good tip for a bellhop in those days, but I tossed the boy a dollar. No sooner had I seated myself in one of the luxurious chairs than the inner voice spoke once more.

"You were restrained from registering in a cheap rooming house because such an environment would have placed you at a great disadvantage in dealing with a publisher. Right now you need an ego-booster, and you are getting it from this finely appointed suite of rooms. Now your mind can conceive on a positive plane that brings success. Ready? Call into your consciousness the name of every person you know who has the financial means to publish your works. When the right name appears, you will recognize it. Get in touch with that person and tell him what you desire."

Without a shred of doubt, in perfect faith, I began to review the names of men who would be able to finance the world's first practical Science of Personal Achievement. After three hours of this my mind went blank. Then a name popped into my mind with such compelling effect that I knew this was the man I wanted. He was Albert Lewis Pelton of Meriden, Connecticut.

All I knew about Mr. Pelton was that he had published a book called *Power of Will*, and that he had advertised this book in my *Golden Rule* magazine several years previously.

Immediately I wrote to Mr. Pelton by Special Delivery. I informed him that I was about to confer upon him the honor of publishing the Science of Personal Achievement.

Two days later I received a telegram saying Mr. Pelton was on his way to Philadelphia to see me. I shall never forget the expression on his face when he was ushered into my suite, nor the words he uttered: "Well, an author who can live in a suite of rooms like this must be the real McCoy!"

The manuscript was about the size of an old-fashioned family Bible. It contained 1800 pages, and weighed about seven pounds. I handed it to Mr. Pelton and he sat down and turned through the pages. After about twenty minutes he closed the book and laid it on the table.

He said: "I will publish this philosophy and pay you the regular author's royalty."

We sent for a typewriter and he typed the contract. At one point he said: "I suppose you'd like an advance on your royalties? I'll make out a check right now." I replied nonchalantly, holding fast to the image my ego had built: "Oh, make it any amount you care to."

"Five hundred dollars?"

"Okay."

Some months later the first published set of my work, *The Law of Success* in eight volumes, was presented to me. Those had been successful months in many ways, for I had regained the power of a positive point of view. I hope sincerely that those who read this story will not have to win their own positive points of view the long way around, as I did.

Had I been guided by some unseen power? I believe some outside force was guiding me. I believe that a mind attuned to currents of faith is attuned beyond its own physical dimension.

Since that eventful day in 1928, I have helped tens of

thousands of men and women to rehabilitate their egos. Most of them I never have met, for our minds contacted each other through the pages of my books. Through my lectures and personal lessons I also have helped many thousands to find the same key to the conceptual and achieving powers of the mind, and here in many cases I had the gratification of seeing it happen.

I have developed a considerable ability to gauge people's needs in this direction and to "press the right button," so to speak. But what takes place when the button is pressed? Whence comes the power that revitalizes a faltering ego? What is it that turns a mind from No to Yes and so opens great gates of accomplishment? I still am seeking that answer. Perhaps the knowledge has been reserved for me to uncover as a sort of post-graduate course in my own work, for I never shall be finished with learning.

Look for your own ego-booster and you will find it. There are amazing varieties of ways to boost the ego. Although they may be mysterious in their inmost essence, their outward manifestations are clear to see. Consider the following examples; they are universal in their application and may help you find your own.

Among the successful insurance men I have trained is one among many who drives an expensive car. His ego-booster is more individual. It consists of a handsome golf bag and set of clubs he carries in full view in his car.

He thus carries with him the impression—both for himself and for others—that he spends considerable time playing golf and is always ready to drive to the links. I do not know if he would be as successful as he is if he did not always display this intimation of success, but I do know that he gets exactly what he needs as an ego-booster.

Another successful insurance agent I trained wears an eight-carat diamond ring which seems to serve as his magic wand as he talks to prospects. This man is one of the largest producers for the Massachusetts Mutual Life Insurance Company.

Once he took his diamond ring to a jeweler for a new mounting. The job required a few days. During those days he worked harder than usual, used every persuasive argument he always had used in order to write a policy, and yet failed to make a sale. He said that when he began to talk to a prospect he would look down for his ring; the ring was not there and somehow he could not put himself over.

When the ring was back on his finger this man went to work as usual, and out of his first six interviews he received six applications for insurance—a record he never had made before.

As for myself, if I were caught in public with such a searchlight on my finger, I would feel so self-conscious that I would get in my own way and be unable to command my ego. To each his own, and a mighty power comes to the man who knows himself!

When a man comes to himself, discovers his ego and takes possession of it, the fact is revealed to the whole world. It is reflected in the tone of his voice, in his facial expression, in the lift of his motions, in the clarity of his thought, in the definiteness of his purpose, in a positive mental attitude that brings out in others the desire to believe in and work with this man.

Friend, when you become commander-in-chief of that very core of your mind, your ego, you are master of all you survey. You never will want, because you will unhesitatingly find the way to plenty. You never will fear, because your mind will not contain fear. You will be free, gloriously free, living a life that pays you in your own terms.

Some few there are who need reins upon their egos. They are so rare, however, that we need not write any part of this book for them.

A healthy ego is a means of health and peace of mind beyond comparison. Look, then, for the one right method or object or condition which helps you to fulfill yourself in "the self-assertive tendency of man."

POINTS TO REMEMBER

1. The self-assertive tendency of man.
2. If you possess a healthy ego, only then will you have peace of mind.
3. Search for your ego-booster.

9

CONCENTRATION

There is a sure way to avoid criticism: be nothing and do nothing. Get a job as a street sweeper and kill off ambition. The remedy never fails.

"You Can Do It if You Believe You Can!"

This lesson occupies a keystone position in this course, for the reason that the psychological law upon which it is based is of vital importance to every other lesson of the course. Let us define the word *concentration*, as it is here used, as follows:

"Concentration is the act of focusing the mind upon a given desire until ways and means for its realization have been worked out and successfully put into operation."

Two important laws enter into the act of *concentrating* the mind on a given *desire*. One is the law of *Auto-suggestion* and the other is the law of *habit*. We will now briefly describe the law of *habit*.

Habit grows out of environment—out of doing the same thing in the same way over and over again—out of repetition—

out of thinking the same thoughts over and over—and, when once formed, it resembles a cement block that has hardened in the mold—in that it is hard to break.

Habit is the basis of all memory training, a fact which you may easily demonstrate in remembering the name of a person whom you have just met, by repeating that name over and over until you have fixed it permanently and plainly in your mind.

> The force of education is so great that we may mold the minds and manners of the young into whatever shape we please and give the impressions of such *habits* as shall ever afterwards remain.
>
> —Atterbury.

Except on rare occasions when the mind rises above environment, the human mind draws the material out of which *thought* is created, from the surrounding environment, and *habit* crystallizes this thought into a permanent fixture and stores it away in the subconscious mind where it becomes a vital part of our personality which silently influences our actions, forms our prejudices and our biases, and controls our opinions.

A great philosopher had in mind the power of *habit* when he said: "We first endure, then pity, and finally embrace," in speaking of the manner in which honest men come to indulge in crime.

Habit may be likened to the grooves on a phonograph record, while the mind may be likened to the needle point that fits into that groove. When any habit has been well formed (by repetition of thought or action) the mind attaches itself to and follows that habit as closely as the phonograph needle follows the groove in the wax record, no matter what may be the nature of that habit.

We begin to see, therefore, the importance of selecting our environment with the greatest of care, because environment is the mental feeding ground out of which the food that goes into our minds is extracted.

Environment very largely supplies the food and materials out of which we create *thought,* and *habit* crystallizes these into permanency. You of course understand that "environment" is the sum total of sources through which you are influenced by and through the aid of the five senses of seeing, hearing, smelling, tasting and feeling.

"Habit is force which is generally recognized by the average thinking person, but which is commonly viewed in its adverse aspect to the exclusion of its favorable phase. It has been well said that all men are 'the creatures of habit,' and that 'habit is a cable; we weave a thread of it each day and it becomes so strong that we cannot break it.'

"If it be true that habit becomes a cruel tyrant, ruling and compelling men against their will, desire, and inclination—and this is true in many cases—the question naturally arises in the thinking mind whether this mighty force cannot be harnessed and controlled in the service of men, just as have other forces of Nature. If this result can be accomplished, then man may master habit and set it to work, instead of being a slave to it and serving it faithfully though complainingly. And the modern psychologists tell us in no uncertain tones that habit may certainly be thus mastered, harnessed and set to work, instead of being allowed to dominate one's actions and character. And thousands of people have applied this new knowledge and have turned the force of habit into new channels, and have compelled it to work their machinery of action, instead of being allowed to run to waste, or else permitted to sweep away the structures that men have erected with care and expense, or to destroy fertile mental fields.

"A habit is a 'mental path' over which our actions have traveled for some time, each passing making the path a little deeper and a little wider. If you have to walk over a field or through a forest, you know how natural it is for you to choose the clearest path in preference to the less worn ones, and greatly in preference to stepping out across the field or through the woods and making a new path. And the line of mental action is precisely the same. It is movement along the lines of least resistance—passage over the well-worn path. Habits are created by repetition and are formed in accordance to a natural law, observable in all animate things and some would say in inanimate things as well. As an instance of the latter, it is pointed out that a piece of paper once folded in a certain way will fold along the same lines the next time. And all users of sewing machines, or other delicate pieces of machinery, know that as a machine or instrument is once 'broken in' so will it tend to run thereafter. The same law is also observable in the case of musical instruments. Clothing or gloves form into creases according to the person using them, and these creases once formed will always be in effect, notwithstanding repeated pressings. Rivers and streams of water cut their courses through the land, and thereafter flow along the habit-course. The law is in operation everywhere.

"These illustrations will help you to form the idea of the nature of habit, and will aid you in forming new mental paths—new mental creases. And—remember this always—the best (and one might say the only) way in which old habits may be removed is to form new habits to counteract and replace the undesirable ones. Form new mental paths over which to travel, and the old ones will soon become less distinct and in time will practically fill up from disuse. Every time you travel over the path of the desirable mental habit, you make the path deeper and wider, and make it so much easier to travel it thereafter. This mental path-making is a very important thing, and I cannot urge upon you too strongly the injunction to start to work making the desirable mental paths over which you wish to travel. Practice, practice, practice—be a good path-maker."

The following are the rules of procedure through which you may form the habits you desire:

First: At the beginning of the formation of a new habit put force and enthusiasm into your expression. Feel what you think. Remember that you are taking the first steps toward making the new mental path; that it is much harder at first than it will be afterwards. Make the path as clear and as deep as you can, at the beginning, so that you can readily see it the next time you wish to follow it.

Second: Keep your attention firmly *concentrated* on the new path-building, and keep your mind away from the old paths, lest you incline toward them. Forget all about the old paths, and concern yourself only with the new ones that you are building to order.

Third: Travel over your newly made paths as often as possible. Make opportunities for doing so, without waiting for them to arise through luck or chance. The oftener you go over the new paths the sooner will they become well worn and easily traveled. Create plans for passing over these new habit-paths, at the very start.

Fourth: Resist the temptation to travel over the older, easier paths that you have been using in the past. Every time you resist a temptation, the stronger do you become, and the easier will it be for you to do so the next time. But every time you yield to the temptation, the easier does it become to yield again, and the more difficult it becomes to resist the next time. You will have a fight on at the start, and this is the critical time. Prove your determination, persistency and willpower now, at the very beginning.

Fifth: Be sure that you have mapped out the right path, as your *definite chief aim,* and then go ahead without fear and without allowing yourself to doubt. "Place your hand upon the plow, and look not backward." Select your goal, then make good, deep, wide mental paths leading straight to it.

As you have already observed, there is a close relationship between *habit* and *Auto-suggestion* (self-suggestion). Through habit, an act repeatedly performed in the same manner has a tendency to become Permanent, and eventually we come to perform the act automatically or unconsciously. In playing a piano, for example, the artist can play a familiar piece while his or her conscious mind is on some other subject.

Auto-suggestion is the tool with which we dig a mental path; Concentration is the hand that holds that tool; and Habit is the map or blueprint which the mental path follows. An idea or desire, to be transformed into terms of action or physical reality, must be held in the conscious mind *faithfully* and *persistently* until *habit* begins to give it permanent form.

Let us turn our attention, now, to *environment.*

As we have already seen, we absorb the material for thought from our surrounding environment. The term "environment" covers a very broad field. It consists of the books we read, the people with whom we associate, the community in which we live, the nature of the work in which we are engaged, the country or nation in which we reside, the clothes we wear, the songs we sing, and, most important of all, *the religious and intellectual training we receive prior to the age of fourteen years.*

The purpose of analyzing the subject of *environment* is to show its direct relationship to the personality we are developing, and the importance of so guarding it that its influence will give us the materials out of which we may attain our *definite chief aim* in life.

The mind feeds upon that which we supply it, or that which is forced upon it, through our *environment;* therefore, let us select our environment, as far as possible, with the object of supplying the mind with suitable material out of which to carry on its work of attaining our *definite chief aim.*

If *your* environment is not to your liking, change it!

The first step is to create in your own mind an exact, clear and well rounded out picture of the environment in which you believe you could best attain your *definite chief aim,* and then *concentrate* your mind upon this picture until you transform it into reality.

The first step you must take, in the accomplishment of any *desire,* is to create in your mind a dear, well defined picture of that which you intend to accomplish. This is the first principle to be observed in your plans for the achievement of *success,* and if you fail or neglect to observe it, you cannot succeed, except by chance.

Your daily associates constitute one of the most important and influential parts of your environment, and may work for your progress or your retrogression, according to the nature of those associates. As far as possible, you should select as your most *intimate* daily associates those who are in sympathy with your aims and ideals—especially those represented by your *definite chief aim*—and whose mental attitude inspires you with enthusiasm, self-confidence, determination and ambition.

Remember that every word spoken within your hearing,

every sight that reaches your eyes, and every sense impression that you receive through any of the five senses, influences your thought as surely as the sun rises in the east and sets in the west. This being true, can you not see the importance of controlling, as far as possible, the environment in which you live and work? Can you not see the importance of reading books that deal with subjects which are directly related to your *definite chief aim?* Can you not see the importance of talking with people who are in sympathy with your aims, and, who will encourage vou and spur you on toward their attainment? We are living in what we call a "twentieth century civilization." The leading scientists of the world are agreed that Nature has been millions of years in creating, through the process of evolution, our present civilized environment.

How many hundreds of centuries the so-called Indians had lived upon the North American continent, without any appreciable advance toward modem civilization, as we understand it, we have no way of ascertaining. Their environment was the wilderness, and they made no attempt whatsoever to change or improve that environment; the change took place only after new races from afar came over and *forced upon them the environment of progressive civilization in, which we are living today.*

DIRECTLY PROPORTIONAL RELATION OF MIND WITH ONE'S SURROUNDINGS

Observe what has happened within the short period of *three centuries.* Hunting grounds have been transformed into great cities, and the Indian has taken on education and culture, in many instances, that equal the accomplishment of his white brothers.

The clothes you wear influence you; therefore, they

constitute a part of your environment. Soiled or shabby clothes depress you and lower your self-confidence, while clean clothes, of an appropriate style, have just the opposite effect.

It is a well-known fact that an observant person can accurately analyze a man by seeing his workbench, desk or other place of employment. A well organized desk indicates a well organized brain. Show me the merchant's stock of goods and I will tell you whether he has an organized or disorganized brain, as there is a close relationship between one's mental attitude and one's physical environment.

The effects of environment so vitally influence those who work in factories, stores and offices, that employers are gradually realizing the importance of creating an environment that inspires and encourages the workers.

One unusually progressive laundryman, in the city of Chicago, has plainly outdone his competitors, by installing in his workroom a player-piano, in charge of a neatly dressed young woman who keeps it going during the working hours. His laundrywomen are dressed in white uniforms, and there is no evidence about the place that work is drudgery. Through the aid of this pleasant environment, this laundryman turns out more work, earns more profits, and pays better wages than his competitors can pay.

This brings us to an appropriate place at which to describe the method through which *you* may apply the principles directly and indirectly related to the subject of *concentration*.

It is the same key that is used, in one form or another, by the followers of New Thought and all other sects which are founded upon the positive philosophy of optimism.

This Magic Key constitutes an irresistible power which all who will may use.

It will unlock the door to riches!

It will unlock the door to fame!

And, in many instances, it will unlock the door to physical health.

It will unlock the door to education and let you into the storehouse of all your latent ability. It will act as a pass-key to any position in life for which you are fitted.

Through the aid of this Magic Key we have unlocked the secret doors to all of the world's great inventions.

Through its magic powers all of our great geniuses of the past have been developed.

Suppose you are a laborer, in a menial position, and desire a better place in life. The Magic Key will help you attain it! Through its use Carnegie, Rockefeller, Hill, Harriman, Morgan and scores of others of their type have accumulated vast fortunes of material wealth.

It will unlock prison doors and turn human derelicts into useful, trustworthy human beings. It will turn failure into success and misery into happiness. You ask—"What is this Magic Key?"

And I answer with one word—*concentration!*

Now let me define *concentration* in the sense that it is here used. First, I wish it to be clearly understood that I have no reference to occultism, although I will admit that all the scientists of the world have failed to explain the strange phenomena produced through the aid of *concentration*.

Concentration, in the sense in which it is here used, means the ability, through fixed habit and practice, to keep your mind on one subject until you have thoroughly familiarized yourself with that subject and mastered it. It means the ability to *control your attention and focus it on a given problem until you have solved it.*

It means the ability to throw off the effects of habits which you wish to discard, and the power to build new habits that are more to your liking. It means complete *self-mastery.*

Stating it in another way, *concentration* is the ability to *think* as you wish to think; the ability to control your thoughts and direct them to a *definite* end; and the ability to organize your knowledge into a plan of action that is sound and workable.

You can readily see that in *concentrating* your mind upon your *definite chief aim* in life, you must cover many closely related subjects which blend into each other and complete the main subject upon which you are concentrating.

Ambition and *desire* are the chief factors which enter into the act of successful *concentration*. Without these factors the Magic Key is useless, and the main reason why so few people make use of this key is that most people lack *ambition,* and *desire nothing in particular.*

Desire whatever you may, and if your desire is within reason and if it is strong enough the Magic Key of *concentration* will help you attain it. There are learned men of science who would have us believe that the wonderful power of prayer operates through the principle of *concentration* on the attainment of a *deeply seated desire.*

Nothing was ever created by a human being which was not first created in the imagination, through *desire,* and then transformed into reality through *concentration.*

Now, let us put the Magic Key to a test, through the aid of a definite formula.

First, you must put your foot on the neck of skepticism and doubt! No unbeliever ever enjoyed the benefits of this Magic Key. You must believe in the test that you are about to make.

We will assume that you have thought something about becoming a successful writer, or a powerful public speaker, or a successful business executive, or an able financier. We will take public speaking as the subject of this test, but remember that you must follow instructions to the letter.

Take a plain sheet of paper, ordinary letter size, and write on it the following:

> I am going to become a powerful public speaker because this will enable me to render the world useful service that is needed—and because it will yield me a financial return that will provide me with the necessary material things of life.
>
> I will concentrate my mind upon this desire for ten minutes daily, just before retiring at night and just after arising in the morning, for the purpose of determining just how I shall proceed to transform it into reality.
>
> I know that I can become a powerful and magnetic speaker, therefore I will permit nothing to interfere with my doing so.
>
> Signed ....

Sign this pledge, then proceed to do as you have pledged your word that you would do. Keep it up until the desired results have been realized.

Now, when you come to do your *concentrating,* this is the way to go about it: Look ahead one, three, five or even ten years, and see yourself as the most powerful speaker of your time. See, in your imagination, an appropriate income. See yourself in your own home that you have purchased with the proceeds from your efforts as a speaker or lecturer. See yourself in possession of a nice bank account as a reserve for old age. See yourself as a person of influence, due to your great ability as a public speaker. See yourself engaged in a life-calling in which you will not fear the loss of your position.

Paint this picture clearly, through the powers of your imagination, and lo! it will soon become transformed into a beautiful picture of deeply seated *desire*. Use this desire as the chief object of your *concentration* and observe what happens.

You now have the secret of the Magic Key!

Do not underestimate the power of the Magic Key because it did not come to you clothed in mysticism, or because it is described in language which all who will may understand. All great truths are simple in final analysis, and easily understood; if they are not they are not *great* truths.

Use this Magic Key with intelligence, and only for the attainment of worthy ends, and it will bring you enduring happiness and success. Forget the mistakes you have made and the failures you have experienced. Quit living in the past, for do you not know that your yesterdays never return? Start all over again, if your previous efforts have not turned out well, and make the next five or ten years tell a story of success that will satisfy your most lofty ambitions.

Make a name for yourself and render the world a great service, through *ambition, desire* and *concentrated effort!*

You can do it if you BELIEVE you can!

Thus endeth the Magic Key.

♦

The presence of any idea or thought in your consciousness tends to produce an "associated" feeling and to urge you to appropriate or corresponding action. Hold a deeply seated *desire* in your consciousness, through the principle of *concentration*, and if you do it with full faith in its realization your act attracts to your aid powers which the entire scientific world has failed to understand or explain with a reasonable hypothesis.

When you become familiar with the powers of *concentration*

you will then understand the reason for choosing a *definite chief aim* as the first step in the attainment of enduring success.

Concentrate your mind upon the attainment of the object of a deeply seated *desire* and very soon you will become a lodestone that attracts, through the aid of forces which no man can explain, the necessary material counterparts of that *desire*, a statement of fact which paves the way for the description of a principle which constitutes the most important part of this lesson, if not, in fact, the most important part of the entire course, viz.:

When two or more people ally themselves, in a spirit of perfect harmony, for the purpose of attaining a definite end, if that alliance is faithfully observed by all of whom it is composed, the alliance brings, to each of those of whom it is composed, power that is superhuman and seemingly irresistible in nature.

ATTAINMENT OF YOUR ZENITH

In chemistry we learn that two or more elements may be so compounded that the result is something entirely different in nature, from any of the individual elements. For example, ordinary water, known in chemistry under the formula of H_2O, is a compound consisting of two atoms of hydrogen and one atom of oxygen, *but water is neither hydrogen nor oxygen.* This "marrying" of elements creates *an entirely different substance from that of either of its component parts.*

The same law through which this transformation of physical elements takes place may be responsible for the seemingly superhuman powers resulting from the alliance of two or more people, *in a perfect state of harmony and understanding*, for the attainment of a given end.

This world, and all matter of which the other planets consist, is made up of electrons (an electron being the smallest known analyzable unit of matter, and resembling, in nature, what we call electricity, or a form of energy). On the other hand, *thought*, and that which we call the "mind," is also a form of energy; in fact it is the highest form of energy known. Thought, in other words, is *organized energy*, and it is not improbable that *thought* is exactly the same sort of energy as that which we generate with an electric dynamo, although of a much more highly *organized* form.

Now, if all matter, in final analysis, consists of groups of electrons, which are nothing more than a form of energy which we call electricity, and if the mind is nothing but a form of highly organized electricity, do you not see how it is possible that the laws which affect matter may also govern the mind?

And if combining two or more elements of matter, in the proper proportion and under the right conditions, will produce something entirely different from those original elements (as in the case of H_2O), do you not see how it is possible so to combine the energy of two or more minds that the result will be a sort of composite mind that is totally different from the individual minds of which it consists?

You have undoubtedly noticed the manner in which; you are influenced while in the presence of other people. Some people inspire you with optimism and enthusiasm. Their very presence seems to stimulate your own mind to greater action, and, this not only "seems" to be true, but it *is true*. You have noticed that the presence of others had a tendency to lower your vitality and depress you; a tendency which I can assure you was very *real!*

What, do you imagine, could be the cause of these changes that come over us when we come within a certain range of other people, unless it is the change resulting from the blending or combining of their minds with our own, through the operation of a law that is not very well understood, but resembles (if, in fact, it is not the same law) the law through which the combining of two atoms of hydrogen and one atom of oxygen produces water.

I have no scientific basis for this hypothesis, but I have given it many years of serious thought and always I come to the conclusion that it is at least a sound hypothesis, although I have no possible way, as yet, of reducing it to a provable hypothesis.

You need no proof, however, that the presence of some people inspires you, while the presence of others depresses you, as you know this to be a fact. Now it stands to reason that the person who inspires you and arouses your mind to a state of greater activity gives you more power to achieve, while the person whose presence depresses you and lowers your vitality, or causes you to *dissipate* it in useless, disorganized thought, has just the opposite effect on you. You can understand this much without the aid of a hypothesis and without further proof than that which you have experienced time after time. Come back, now, to the original statement that:

"When two or more people ally themselves, *in a spirit of perfect harmony,* for the purpose of attaining a definite end, if that alliance is *faithfully observed by all of whom it is composed,* the alliance brings, to each of those of whom it is composed, power that is superhuman and seemingly irresistible in nature."

Study, closely, the emphasized part of the foregoing statement, for there you will find the "mental formula" which, if not faithfully observed, destroys the effect of the whole.

One atom of hydrogen combined with one atom of oxygen will not produce water, nor will an alliance in name only, that is not accompanied by *"a spirit of perfect harmony"* (between those forming the alliance), produce *"power that is superhuman and seemingly irresistible in nature."*

I have in mind a family of mountain-folk who, for more than six generations, have lived in the mountainous section of Kentucky. Generation after generation of this family came and went without any noticeable improvement of a mental nature, each generation following in the footsteps of its ancestors. They made their living from the soil, and as far as they knew, or cared, the universe consisted of a little spot of territory known as Letcher County. They married strictly in their own "set," and in their own community.

Finally, one of the members of this family strayed away from the flock, so to speak, and married a well educated and highly cultured woman from the neighbor-state of Virginia. This woman was one of those types of ambitious people who had learned that the universe extended beyond the border line of Letcher County, and covered, at least, the whole of the southern states. She had heard of chemistry, and of botany, and of biology, and of pathology, and of psychology, and of many other subjects that were of importance in the field of education. When her children began to come along to the age of understanding, she talked to them of these subjects; and they, in turn, began to show a keen interest in them.

One of her children is now the president of a great educational institution, where most of these subjects, and many others of equal importance, are taught. Another one of them is a prominent lawyer, while still another is a successful physician.

Her husband (thanks to the influence of her mind) is a well-known dental surgeon, and the first of his family, for six generations, to break away from the traditions by which the family had been bound.

The blending of her mind with his *gave him the needed stimulus to spur him on and inspired him with ambition such as he would never have known without her influence.*

For many years I have been studying the biographies of those whom the world calls *great*, and it seems to me more than a mere coincidence that in every instance where the facts were available the person who was really responsible for the *greatness* was in the background, behind the scenes, and seldom heard of by the hero-worshiping public. Not infrequently is this "hidden power" a patient little wife who has inspired her husband and urged him on to great achievement, as was true in the case I have just described.

Henry Ford is one of the modem miracles of this age, and I doubt that this country, or any other, ever produced an industrial genius of his equal. If the *facts* were known (and perhaps they are known) they might trace the cause of Mr. Ford's phenomenal achievements to a woman of whom the public hears but little—*his wife!*

We read of Ford's achievements and of his enormous income and imagine him to be blessed with matchless ability; and he is—ability of which the world would never have heard had it not been for the modifying influence of his wife, who has co-operated with him, during all the years of his struggle, *"in a spirit of perfect harmony, for the purpose of attaining a definite end."*

When two or more people ally themselves, *"in a spirit of perfect harmony, for the purpose of attaining a definite end,"* the *end*, itself, or the *desire* back of that end, may be likened to the apple seed, and the blending of the forces of energy of the two or more minds may be likened to the air and the soil out of which come the elements that form the material objects of that *desire*.

The *power* back of the attraction and combination of these forces of the mind can no more be explained than can the power back of the combination of elements out of which an apple tree "grows."

But the all-important thing is that an apple tree will "grow" from a seed thus properly planted, and great *achievement* will follow the systematic blending of two or more minds with a definite object in view.

POINTS TO REMEMBER

1. The law of auto-suggestion and the law of habit are necessary in order to learn how to concentrate well.
2. Habit is the basis of cultivating a good memory.
3. Setting up a definite chief aim is the most important step towards attaining success.

10

THE HABIT OF SAVING

"Man is a combination of fleshy bone, blood, hair and brain cells. These are the building materials out of which he shapes, through the Law of Habit, his own personality."

To advise one to save money without describing how to save would be somewhat like drawing the picture of a horse and writing under it, "This is a horse." It is obvious to all that the saving of money is one of the essentials for success, but the big question uppermost in the minds of the majority of those who do not save is:

"How can I do it?"

The saving of money is solely a matter of *habit*. For this reason this lesson begins with a brief analysis of the Law of Habit.

It is literally true that man, through the Law of Habit, shapes his own personality. Through repetition, any act indulged in a few times becomes a habit, and the mind appears to be nothing more than a mass of motivating forces growing out of our daily habits.

When once fixed in the mind a habit voluntarily impels one to action. For example, follow a given route to your daily work, or to some other place that you frequently visit, and very soon the habit has been formed and your mind will lead you over that route without thought on your part. Moreover, if you start out with the intention of traveling in another direction, without keeping the thought of the change in routes constantly in mind, you will find yourself following the old route.

Public speakers have found that the telling over and over again of a story, which may be based upon pure fiction, brings into play the Law of Habit, and very soon they forget whether the story is true or not.

WALLS OF LIMITATION BUILT THROUGH HABIT

Millions of people go through life in poverty and want because they have made destructive use of the Law of Habit. Not understanding either the Law of Habit or the Law of Attraction through which "like attracts like," those who remain in poverty seldom realize that they are where they are as the result of their own acts.

Fix in your mind the thought that your ability is limited to a given earning capacity and you will never earn more than that, because the law of habit will set up a definite limitation of the amount you can earn, your subconscious mind will accept this limitation, and very soon you will feel yourself "slipping" until finally you will become so hedged in by FEAR OF POVERTY (one of the six basic fears) that opportunity will no longer knock at your door; your doom will be sealed; your fate fixed.

Formation of the Habit of Saving does not mean that you shall limit your earning capacity; it means just the opposite—that you shall apply this law so that it not only conserves that which you earn, in a systematic manner, but it also places you in the way of greater opportunity and gives you the vision, the self-confidence, the imagination, the enthusiasm, the initiative and leadership actually to increase your earning capacity.

One of the most successful bankers in the state of Illinois has this sign hanging in his private office:

"WE TALK AND THINK ONLY OF ABUNDANCE HERE. IF YOU HAVE A TALE OF WOE PLEASE KEEP IT, AS WE: DO NOT WANT IT."

No business firm wants the services of a pessimist, and those who understand the Law of Attraction and the Law of Habit will no more tolerate the pessimist than they would permit a burglar to roam around their place of business, for the reason that one such person will destroy the usefulness of those around him.

In tens of thousands of homes the general topic of conversation is poverty and want, and that is just what they are getting. They think of poverty, they talk of poverty, they accept poverty as their lot in life. They reason that because their ancestors were poor before them they, also, must remain poor.

The poverty consciousness is formed as the result of the habit of thinking of and fearing poverty. "Lo! The thing I had feared has come upon me."

THE SLAVERY OF DEBT

Debt is a merciless master, a fatal enemy of the savings habit.

Poverty, alone, is sufficient to kill off ambition, destroy self-confidence and destroy hope, but add to it the burden of debt and all who are victims of these two cruel task-masters are practically doomed to failure.

No man can do his best work, no man can express himself in terms that command respect, no man can either create or carry out a definite purpose in life, with heavy debt hanging over his head. The man who is bound in the slavery of debt is just as helpless as the slave who is bound by ignorance, or by actual chains. The author has a very close friend whose income is $1,000 a month. His wife loves "society" and tries to make a $20,000 showing on a $12,000 income, with the result that this poor fellow is usually about $8,000 in debt. Every member of his family has the "spending habit," having acquired this from the mother. The children, two girls and one boy, are now of the age when they are thinking of going to college, but this is impossible because of the father's debts. The result is dissension between the father and his children which makes the entire family unhappy and miserable.

It is a terrible thing even to think of going through life like a prisoner in chains, bound down and owned by somebody else on account of debts. The accumulation of debts is a habit. It starts in a small way and grows to enormous proportions slowly, step by step, until finally it takes charge of one's very soul.

Thousands of young men start their married lives with unnecessary debts hanging over their heads and never manage to get out from under the load. After the novelty of marriage begins to wear off (as it usually does) the married couple begin to feel the embarrassment of want, and this feeling grows until it leads, oftentimes, to open dissatisfaction with one another, and eventually to the divorce court.

A man who is bound by the slavery of debt has no time or inclination to set up or work out ideals, with the result that he drifts downward with time until he eventually begins to set up limitations in his own mind, and by these he hedges himself behind prison walls of FEAR and doubt from which he never escapes. No sacrifice is too great to avoid the misery of debt!

"Think of what you owe yourself and those who are dependent upon you and resolve to be no man's debtor," is the advice of one very successful man whose early chances were destroyed by debt. This man came to himself soon enough to throw off the habit of buying that which he did not need and eventually worked his way out of slavery.

Most men who develop the habit of debt will not be so fortunate as to come to their senses in time to save themselves, because debt is something like quicksand in that it has a tendency to draw its victim deeper and deeper into the mire.

The Fear of Poverty is one of the most destructive of the six basic fears described in Lesson Three. The man who becomes hopelessly in debt is seized with this poverty fear, his ambition and self-confidence become paralyzed, and he sinks gradually into oblivion.

There are two classes of debts, and these are so different in nature that they deserve to be here described, as follows:

1. There are debts incurred for luxuries which become a dead loss.
2. There are debts incurred in the course of professional or business trading which represent service or merchandise that can be converted back into assets.

The first class of debts is the one to be avoided. The second class may be indulged in, providing the one incurring the debts uses judgment and does not go beyond the bounds of reasonable limitation. The moment one buys beyond his limitations he enters the realm of speculation, and speculation swallows more of its victims than it enriches.

Practically all people who live beyond their means are

tempted to speculate with the hope that they may recoup, at a single turn of the wheel of fortune, so to speak, their entire indebtedness. The wheel generally stops at the wrong place and, far from finding themselves out of debt, such people as indulge in speculation are bound more closely as slaves of debt.

The Fear of Poverty breaks down the willpower of its victims, and they then find themselves unable to restore their lost fortunes, and, what is still more sad, they lose all ambition to extricate themselves from, the slavery of debt.

Hardly a day passes that one may not see an account in the newspapers of at least one suicide as the result of worry over debts. The slavery of debt causes more suicides every year than all other causes combined, which is a slight indication of the cruelty of the poverty fear.

During the war millions of men faced the front-line trenches without flinching, knowing that death might overtake them any moment. Those same men, when facing the Fear of Poverty, often cringe and out of sheer desperation, which paralyzes their reason, sometimes commit suicide.

The person who is free from debt may whip poverty and achieve outstanding financial success, but, if he is bound by debt, such achievement is but a remote possibility, and never a probability.

Fear of Poverty is a negative, destructive state of mind. Moreover, one negative state of mind has a tendency to attract other similar states of mind. For example, the Fear of Poverty may attract the fear of Ill Health, and these two may attract the Fear of Old Age, so that the victim finds himself poverty-stricken, in ill health and actually growing old long before the time when he should begin to show the signs of old age. Millions of untimely, nameless graves have been filled by this cruel state of mind known as the Fear of Poverty!

Less than a dozen years ago a young man held a responsible position with the City National Bank, of New York City. Through living beyond his income he contracted a large amount of debts which caused him to worry until this destructive habit began to show up in his work and he was dismissed from the bank's service.

He secured another position, at less money, but his creditors embarrassed him so that he decided to resign and go away into another city, where he hoped to escape them until he had accumulated enough money to pay off his indebtedness. Creditors have a way of tracing debtors, so very soon they were close on the heels of this young man, whose employer found out about his indebtedness and dismissed him from his position.

He then searched in vain for employment for two months. One cold night he went to the top of one of the tall buildings on Broadway and jumped off. Debt had claimed another victim.

HOW TO MASTER THE FEAR OF POVERTY

To whip the Fear of Poverty one must take two very definite steps, providing one is in debt. First, quit the habit of buying on credit, and follow this by gradually paying off the debts that you have already incurred.

Being free from the worry of indebtedness you are ready to revamp the habits of your mind and redirect your course toward prosperity. Adopt, as a part of your Definite Chief Aim, the habit of saving a regular proportion of your income, even if this be no more than a penny a day. Very soon this habit will begin to lay hold of your mind and you will actually get joy out of saving.

Any habit may be discontinued by building in its place some other and more desirable habit. The "spending" habit must be replaced by the "saving" habit by all who attain financial independence.

Merely to discontinue an undesirable habit is not enough, as such habits have a tendency to reappear unless the place they formerly occupied in the mind is filled by some other habit of a different nature.

The discontinuance of a habit leaves a "hole" in the mind, and this hole must be filled up with some other form of habit or the old one will return and claim its place.

It is assumed that you are striving to attain financial independence. The accumulation of money is not difficult after you have once mastered the Fear of Poverty and developed in its place the Habit of Saving.

The author of this course would be greatly disappointed to know that any student of the course got the impression from anything in this or any of the other lessons that Success is measured by dollars alone.

However, money does represent an important factor in success, and it must be given its proper value in any philosophy intended to help people in becoming useful, happy and prosperous.

The cold, cruel, relentless truth is that in this age of materialism, a man is no more than so many grains of sand, which may be blown helter-skelter by every stray wind of circumstance, unless he is entrenched behind the power of money!

Genius may offer many rewards to those who possess it, but the fact still remains that genius without money with which to give it expression is but an empty, skeleton-like honor.

The man without money is at the mercy of the man who has it!

And this goes, regardless of the amount of ability he may possess, the training he has had or the native genius with which he was gifted by nature.

There is no escape from the fact that people will weigh you very largely in the light of bank balances, no matter who you are or what you can do. The first question that arises, in the minds of most people, when they meet a stranger, is, "How much money has he?" If he has money he is welcomed into homes and business opportunities are thrown his way. All sorts of attention are lavished upon him. He is a prince, and as such is entitled to the best of the land.

But if his shoes are run down at the heels, his clothes are not pressed, his collar is dirty, and he shows plainly the signs of impoverished finances, woe be his lot, for the passing crowd will step on his toes and blow the smoke of disrespect in his face.

These are not pretty statements, but they have one virtue— THEY ARE TRUE!

This tendency to judge people by the money they have, or their power to control money, is not confined to any one class of people. We all have a touch of it, whether we recognize the fact or not.

Thomas A. Edison is one of the best known and most respected inventors in the world, yet it is no misstatement of facts to say that he would have remained a practically unknown, obscure personage had he not followed the habit of conserving his resources and shown his ability to save money.

Henry Ford never would have got to first base with his "horseless carriage" had he not developed, quite early in life, the habit of saving. Moreover, had Mr. Ford not conserved his resources and hedged himself behind their power he would have been "swallowed up" by his competitors or those who covetously desired to take his business away from him, long, long years ago.

Many a man has gone a very long way toward success, only to stumble and fall, never again to rise, because of lack of money in times of emergency. The mortality rate in business each year, due to lack of reserve capital for emergencies, is stupendous. To this one cause are due more of the business failures than to all other causes combined!

Reserve Funds are essential in the successful operation of business!

Likewise, Savings Accounts are essential to success on the part of individuals. Without a savings fund the individual suffers in two ways: first, by inability to seize opportunities that come only to the person with some ready cash, and, second, by embarrassment due to some unexpected emergency calling for cash.

It might be said, also, that the individual suffers in still a third respect by not developing the Habit of Saving, through lack of certain other qualities essential for success which grow out of the practice of the Habit of Saving.

The nickels, dimes and pennies which the average person allows to slip through his fingers would, if systematically saved and properly put to work, eventually bring financial independence.

HOW MUCH SHOULD ONE SAVE?

The first question that will arise is, "How Much Should One Save?" The answer cannot be given in a few words, for the amount one should save depends upon many conditions, some of which may be within one's control and some of which may not be.

Generally speaking, a man who works for a salary should apportion his income about as follows:

Savings Account	20%
Living—Clothes, Food and Shelter	50%
Education	10%
Recreation	10%
Life Insurance	10%
	100%

The following, however, indicates the approximate distribution which the average man actually makes of his income:

Savings Account	Nothing
Living—Clothes, Food and Shelter	60%
Education	0%
Recreation	35%
Life Insurance	5%
	100%

Under the item of "recreation" is included, of course, many expenditures that do not really "recreate," such as money spent for alcoholic drinks, dinner parties and other similar items which may actually serve to undermine one's health and destroy character.

An experienced analyst of men has stated that he could tell very accurately, by examining a man's monthly budget, what sort of a life the man is living; moreover, that he will get most of his information from the one item of "recreation." This, then, is an item to be watched as carefully as the greenhouse keeper watches the thermometer which controls the life and death of his plants.

Those who keep budget accounts often include an item

called "entertainment," which, in a majority of cases, turns out to be an evil because it depletes the income heavily and when carried to excess depletes, also, the health. We are living, right now, in an age when the item of "entertainment" is altogether too high in most budget allowances. Tens of thousands of people who earn not more than $50.00 a week are spending as much as one third of their incomes for what they call "entertainment," which comes in a bottle, with a questionable label on it, at anywhere from $6.00 to $12.00 a quart. Not only are these unwise people wasting the money that should go into a savings fund, but, of far greater danger, they are destroying both character and health.

Nothing in this lesson is intended as a preachment on morality, or on any other subject. We are here dealing with cold facts which, to a large extent, constitute the building materials out of which SUCCESS may be created.

However, this is an appropriate place to state some FACTS which have such a direct bearing on the subject of achieving success that they cannot be omitted without weakening this entire course in general and this lesson in particular.

We are all victims of HABIT!

Unfortunately for most of us, we are reared by parents who have no conception whatsoever of the psychology of habit, and, without being aware of their fault, most parents aid and abet their offspring in the development of the spending habit by overindulgence with spending money, and by lack of training in the Habit of Saving.

The habits of early childhood cling to us all through life.

Fortunate, indeed, is the child whose parents have the foresight and the understanding of the value, as a character builder, of the Habit of Saving, to inculcate this habit in the minds of their children.

It is a training that yields rich rewards.

Give the average man $100.00 that he did not contemplate receiving, and what will he do with it? Why, he will begin to cogitate in his own mind on how he can SPEND the money. Dozens of things that he needs, or THINKS he needs, will flash into his mind, but it is a rather safe bet that it will never occur to him (unless he has acquired the savings habit) to make this $100.00 the beginning of a savings account. Before night comes he will have the $100.00 spent, or at least he will have decided in his mind how he is going to SPEND IT, thus adding more fuel to the already too bright flame of Habit of Spending.

We are ruled by our habits!

It requires force of character, determination and power of firm DECISION to open a savings account and then add to it a regular, if small, portion of all subsequent income.

There is one rule by which any man may determine, well in advance, whether or not he will ever enjoy the financial freedom and independence which is so universally desired by all men, and this rule has absolutely nothing to do with the amount of one's income.

The rule is that if a man follows the systematic habit of saving a definite proportion of all money he earns or receives in other ways, he is practically sure to place himself in a position of financial independence. If he saves nothing, he IS ABSOLUTELY SURE NEVER TO BE FINANCIALLY INDEPENDENT, no matter how much his income may be.

The one and only exception to this rule is that a man who does not save might possibly inherit such a large sum of money that he could not spend it, or he might inherit it under a trust which would protect it for him, but these eventualities are rather remote; so much so, in fact, that YOU cannot rely upon such a miracle happening to you.

POINTS TO REMEMBER

1. Develop the mindset to make saving money a habit.
2. The poverty consciousness is formed as the result of the habit of thinking of and fearing poverty.
3. Beware of the merciless trap of debt.

11

CULTIVATE CREATIVE VISION

Creative vision requires you to stimulate your imagination to work toward your definite major purpose and to put the results of that imagination to work.

Expressed by people unafraid of criticism, creative vision is responsible for the shape of civilization today. It has brought every advancement in thought, science, and mechanics that allows our current standard of living. It inspires you to pioneer and experiment with new ideas in every field. It is always on the lookout for better ways of doing things.

Creative vision belongs only to people who have the habit of going the extra mile, for it recognizes no nine-to-five working hours and it isn't concerned with monetary rewards. Its aim is doing the impossible.

This chapter will give you great examples of creative vision and show you how to understand the process by which it works so that you can apply it in your own life.

SYNTHETIC IMAGINATION

Imagination, like reasoning, takes two forms: synthetic and creative imagination. Each can contribute to the betterment of your own life and the world around you through creative vision.

Synthetic imagination combines previously recognized ideas, concepts, plans, or facts in a new way or puts them to new use.

An excellent example of synthetic imagination is Edison's invention of the lightbulb. He began with one recognized fact that other people had discovered: A wire could be heated by electricity until it produced light. The problem was that the intense heat quickly burned the wire out. The light never lasted more than a few minutes.

Edison failed more than ten thousand times in his attempt to control this heat. When he found the method, it was by applying another common fact which had simply eluded everyone else. He realized that charcoal is produced by setting wood on fire, covering it with soil, and allowing the fire to smolder until the wood is charred. The soil permits only enough air to reach the fire to keep it burning without blazing.

When Edison recognized this fact, his imagination immediately associated it with the idea of heating the wire. He placed the wire inside a bottle, pumped out most of the air, and produced the first incandescent light. It burned for eight and a half hours.

Edison's creative vision depended on several important principles of the science of personal achievement. He applied the habit of going the extra mile because he labored without immediate pay. He worked with definiteness of purpose and was inspired by applied faith to carry on with his work through an incredible number of failures that would have broken most people.

Finally he applied the mastermind principle by assembling a team of skilled chemists and mechanics to perfect his invention, finding the right kind and thickness of wire, the right quantity of air to leave in the bulb, the best way to construct the bulb, so that his invention took on the most efficient form possible.

Synthetic imagination does not depend on having tremendous personal advantages. Edison had spent only three months in grade school, had supported himself for many years as a telegrapher, and was fired from almost every job he held. He began to lose his hearing early on and eventually became almost completely deaf. But he turned his life around through definiteness of purpose, the habit of going the extra mile, and applied faith.

Thomas Stemberg was a successful executive in the grocery business. Working with a Connecticut-based chain, he opened a string of high-volume mega supermarkets that offered consumers huge selections at low prices.

The stores were very successful, and Stemberg was building a sterling reputation in his business. But he wasn't satisfied. He saw the prosperous grocery megastores and wondered if the megastore concept couldn't be applied to something else.

He wanted to start a large business in a big market underserved by modern distribution methods, offering customers a good value. He formed a mastermind alliance with Leo Kahn, the man who had pioneered the grocery megastores, and in 1986 he opened Staples, the first mega-business-supply store.

Stemberg's idea was so smart, so right that it immediately inspired competitors like Office Depot and OfficeMax, to revolutionize the business supply industry. Despite the competition, Staples surpassed even Stemberg's ambitious expectations. In just seven years sales exceeded one billion dollars. Thomas Stemberg didn't invent the superstore idea, but he applied it to a market that had been quiet and humdrum for decades. He developed a definite plan for attaining his goal; he formed a mastermind alliance with Kahn, the man who understood the concept best; he put his plan into action with applied faith; and he went the extra mile by offering customers more and better service than they could get anywhere else.

Synthetic imagination puts the entire sum of human knowledge at your disposal, but like any other part of the science of success, it requires your dedication to making your vision into reality.

CREATIVE IMAGINATION

Creative imagination has its base in the subconscious. It is the medium through which you recognize new ideas and newly learned facts. All your efforts to impress your definite major purpose on your subconscious work to stimulate your creative imagination.

F. W. Woolworth was working as a clerk in a hardware store. He was, at that point, simply determined to be a good and valuable employee. When his boss complained about piles of out-of-date goods that weren't selling, Woolworth's imagination went to work.

"I can sell those items," he told his boss, and with his employer's permission, he set up a table in the store, laid out all of the dud merchandise, and priced everything at ten cents. The stock sold remarkably fast, and soon the owner was searching for anything he could lay his hands on to put on that table, which became the most profitable spot in the store.

Woolworth had the faith to apply his new idea to an entire store; his boss didn't. The Woolworth chain of five-and-dimes quickly spread across the nation, earning him a fortune. His former boss once commented, "Every word I used in turning that man's offer down has cost me about a million dollars I might have earned."

Woolworth was so committed to his then-modest purpose of being a valuable employee that his imagination was ready to back up his commitment with powerful ideas. He certainly went the extra mile for his boss, but because that man didn't have the vision that Woolworth had, other investors formed Woolworth's mastermind alliance and profited from it.

CREATIVE VISION GOES BEYOND IMAGINATION

Creative vision is more than an interest in material things; it is a commitment to a better future. Synthetic imagination springs from experience and reason; creative imagination springs from your commitment to your definite purpose. Creative vision depends heavily upon creative imagination, but it is also more than that.

Imagination recognizes limitations, handicaps, and opposition; creative vision rides over these as if they did not exist, for it has its base in Infinite Intelligence.

One of the purest examples I know of creative vision is illustrated by the story of Dr. Elmer Gates. Gates was an inventor who worked at the same time as Edison, but his methods and background were very different. He was a highly trained scientist, and his patents actually outnumbered Edison's two to one.

Gates applied creative vision in a remarkably simple process. He would enter a soundproof room, sit down at a table with pencil and paper, and turn off the lights. He then concentrated his thoughts on a particular problem and waited for the ideas that he needed for its solution.

Sometimes ideas flowed to Gates immediately; sometimes he had to wait for as much as an hour before they came. Occasionally nothing happened. At other times he perceived solutions to other problems that he hadn't even been thinking about.

Dr. Gates's creative vision transcended imagination because he had developed it into a faculty he could call upon at will. Creative vision produces results, not alibis.

CREATIVE VISION IS NEEDED TODAY

There are countless calls for creative vision in the world today.

1. We need forms of energy that do not pollute or drain our environment.
2. We need schools that capture the attention of our young people and teach them to better themselves.
3. We need cures and vaccines for terrible diseases that threaten the earth's people.
4. We need people who can show small business how to use and profit from rapidly changing technology.
5. We need plans for controlling the cost of health care and making it affordable for every honest worker without destroying the incentive of the professionals who provide it.

There is both challenge and opportunity in these needs, and I raise them only to start you thinking about the scope of the possibilities for creative vision.

There is a place in America for every person who can render any type of useful service and is willing to render it with the right mental attitude. If you have creative vision, you will recognize this and profit from it. You will never complain of a lack of opportunity.

Great leaders of every generation in this country began their careers in humble occupations. Andrew Carnegie was a bobbin boy in a textile mill. W. Clement Stone was a newsboy. Harry Truman was a haberdasher. Ruth Bader Ginsburg had to become a law secretary when she graduated from law school because judges couldn't imagine hiring a woman clerk, yet now she sits on the Supreme Court.

It makes little difference where you begin. The important thing to ask is: Where are you going? What motive inspires you to give your best? Are you willing to go the extra mile? Are you a clock-watcher, eager for the day to end? Or do you look for the opportunity to make yourself indispensable to others?

These are the questions you must ask yourself. If you have creative vision, you can answer them. You know where you are going, you know what you desire, and you know that life never lets you get something for nothing without eventually forcing you to pay more for it than it is worth.

When you have creative vision, you know that you can succeed only by helping others to succeed, and you know that it isn't necessary for anyone to fail in the process.

Creative vision lets you make decisions quickly. And it lets you change those decisions as soon as you realize a mistake has been made. It frees you from fear of others, for it makes you feel at peace with yourself in your knowledge that you are fair and honest.

It's a common human trait to envy people who have attained success, looking at them only in the moments of their triumph and forgetting the prices they had to pay. Often we suspect that they owe their success to some sort of pull, luck, or dishonesty.

But creative vision makes you keenly aware of the price of personal achievement because you yourself know its labors. You understand the benefits of sharing your blessings, experiences, and opportunities with others; you know that your success actually depends on it.

If you feel the need for a creative vision in your life, you can begin to develop it by getting on better terms with your own conscience, inspiring yourself with greater self-reliance, providing yourself with a definite major purpose, and keep going.

POINTS TO REMEMBER

1. Significance of a creative vision today.
2. Be keenly aware at what cost personal achievement is attained.
3. Your eagerness to go the extra mile is what separates you from others.

12

PEACE OF MIND AND POWER OF MIND

Since what you achieve in life depends on what you first conceive, and this depends first of all upon your deep, inner, subconsciously founded belief—you see that your life depends upon your power to believe.

No, your mere life-processes do not depend upon this power. The Eternal has made it possible for the supreme achievement of evolution, man, to stay alive even without knowing he is alive. The beating of the heart, the pumping of the lungs, the processes of digestion and other vital functions are taken care of by a part of the brain which takes care of itself.

Beyond this, man creates an ever better species. He aspires—and climbs to the heights of his aspiration. Seeing heights yet beyond, again he aspires—and achieves that peak, beyond which lies another and another.

Significantly, philosophers always have recognized the power of the quiet mind, the peaceful mind. This is far from being a mind empty of aspiration. It is, rather, a mind which can hold, judge and evaluate the highest forms of aspiration. Nor is a peaceful mind the exclusive property of a person who does not move about in the world and busy himself with the world's manifold affairs, for some of the most peaceful minds are the busiest. Remember, we speak of inner peace, like a quiet center about which all else revolves, like a great rotating dynamo doing useful work and filled with energy, yet referring its rotation always to the unmoved pivot at its middle.

A mind at peace is a mind that is free to conceive greatly. It bears no great conflict within its subconscious which may hamper the conscious mind and therefore conscious action. A mind at peace is a free mind. Its power is limitless.

POINTS TO REMEMBER

1. Your life depends on your power to believe.
2. The power that lies behind a quiet and peaceful mind.
3. A mind at peace is a mind that is free to conceive greatly.

www.ingramcontent.com/pod-product-compliance
Lightning Source LLC
Chambersburg PA
CBHW021158160426
43194CB00007B/788